GALATI

A Call

L.

GALATIANS

A Call to Christian Liberty

by

HOWARD F. VOS

MOODY PRESS

CHICAGO

NOTE: The author has translated Galatians from the original Greek and has employed this translation in his commentary.

Library of Congress Catalog Card Number: 77-123159

ISBN: 0-8024-2048-6

15 16 17 Printing/EP/Year 91 90 89 88

Printed in the United States of America

CONTENTS

CONTENTS

BACKGROUNDS AND OUTLINE

Contemporary Western man—especially American man —prides himself on personal freedom. He has much to say about the guarantees of the Bill of Rights in terms of freedom of religion (or freedom for no religion), of speech, of press and assembly. He frequently appeals to the Declaration of Independence and "natural rights" with which all men are endowed. But especially he follows "the new look" in Christian ethics, or "the new morality," or ethics in "a new key," or "situation ethics" as portrayed by Joseph Fletcher, Harvey Cox, John A. T. Robinson, and others. He welcomes the revolution in morals taking place in Western society, joins free speech and free love societies, and claims that an ethical decision is to be determined by an individual reacting to a concrete situation rather than on the basis of claims of an abstract conception of right such as found in Scripture.

For a generation that puts much stress on personal freedom, the book of Galatians seems to have a contemporary relevance. Its message is liberty—freedom from the law. Such a thought appeals to those who seek to lift all kinds of personal and moral restraint in our day. But Galatians does not encourage that kind of liberty. In asserting freedom from the law, it underscores the fact that salvation is

in no way based on human effort. Nor is the Christian life
a succession of inhibitions. Rather, Galatians teaches that
Christ fulfilled the law and provided the means of salvation. Now He resides within the one who has been justified by faith to supply the kind of power needed to live
the Christian life.

The contemporary relevance of Galatians, then, is that
it attacks the ever present desire of men to achieve salvation by their own efforts and the tendency of Christians
to live the Christian life in their own strength or in a legalistic way. In stressing Christian liberty, Galatians does
not open the door to lawlessness. It encourages believers
not to be weary in welldoing (Gal 6:9) and reminds them
that what a man sows he shall reap (v. 7). In short, the
book admonishes believers to live by the power of the
Holy Spirit and to walk in the Spirit (5:16, 25). Further,
Paul in this epistle makes it quite clear that the believer
who seeks to live the Christian life in his own strength
or in a legalistic fashion does not enjoy the power of the
Holy Spirit to free him from his sinful self so he can live
well-pleasing to God.

The small epistle to the Galatians has played a significant part in the history of the church and indeed of the
entire Western world. In the early church it heralded a
clarion call for the distinctiveness of Christianity with its
message of justification by faith. Tenney declares, "Christianity might have been just one more Jewish sect, and the
thought of the Western world might have been entirely
pagan had it never been written."[1] Luther's *Commentary
on Galatians* was the manifesto of the Protestant Reformation and its message the major theme of Reformation

preaching. And Galatians has a relevant message of justification by faith for modern man, with all his cults and religious systems that seek to gain heaven by good works.

THE WRITER

In the very first verse the apostle Paul claims to have
written this epistle to the Galatian Christians. Not only
does he claim authorship, he asserts apostolic authority for
the contents. Paul's name is not merely an arbitrary inser-
tion by a forger in chapter 1, because it appears again in
5:2. Moreover, the apostle's personality shines through the
entire message; and most of the first two chapters are au-
tobiographical in nature. So general was the acceptance
of Paul's authorship of Galatians in the early church that
even the heretic Marcion acknowledged the book to be
Pauline in his mid-second-century New Testament canon.
And when the Tubingen school of higher criticism began
to question the authorship of the Pauline epistles during
the last century, it did not deny the apostle's composition
of Galatians. So few and so weak have been the questioning voices that it may be said that no real doubt exists as
to the Pauline authorship of Galatians today.

THE CHURCHES ADDRESSED

According to Galatians 1:2, the epistle was addressed to
"the churches of Galatia." But the location of these
churches has been considerably debated. By way of background, it may be noted that the Galatians, or Gauls, or
Celts, moved down through Italy and terrorized Rome in
390 B.C. Sacking the city, they moved back northward and
threatened the Romans from their Po Valley bases for

many decades thereafter. In the latter part of the third century some of these people joined with Hannibal in his effort to destroy Roman power. Meanwhile, not long after 300 B.C., another group of Gauls (Galatians) descended on Greece, where they were defeated at Delphi. Then they set up a small kingdom in Thrace, from which they invaded Asia Minor in 278-277 B.C. After much raiding and plundering they were penned in in an area of north central Asia Minor by Attalus I of Pergamum about 230 B.C., and they gave their name to the area.

For the next forty years they continued to harass their neighbors until 189, when they were defeated by the Romans but were permitted to retain their independence. Henceforth the Galatians remained loyal to Rome and in 64 B.C. became a client kingdom of Rome. At that time the territory was organized on the Celtic tribal basis; three tribes occupied separate areas with their respective capitals at Pessinus, Ancyra (modern Ankara), and Tavium. From 44 B.C. Galatia was under only one ruler, and King Amyntas rose to power there under the sponsorship of Mark Antony. Subsequently Rome added various portions of southern Asia Minor to his kingdom.

His government was so effective in pacifying the area that when he died in 25 B.C. and bequeathed his kingdom to Rome, he left it in such an excellent state that Rome incorporated it into the Empire as the province of Galatia. The province of Galatia then included besides Galatia proper (in north central Asia Minor), parts of Phrygia, Lycaonia, Pisidia, and Pamphylia (in south central Asia Minor), and occupied approximately the central third of Asia Minor. It remained in this form until about A.D. 72

when additional increases in its territory were made. The two principal cities of the province of Galatia were Ancyra (the metropolis) and Pisidian Antioch. In width the Galatian province varied from 100 to 175 miles; it was some 250 miles from north to south.

It may be readily seen that "Galatia" could refer either in an ethnic sense to a territory in north central Asia Minor or in a political sense to the province of Galatia. Questions often arise as to the sense in which Luke and Paul used the term and to whom Paul wrote when he penned the epistle to the Galatians. Was he writing to believers in the northern part of the province of Galatia (probably in Pessinus, Ancyra, and Tavium) or to churches in Derbe, Lystra, Iconium, and Antioch in the southern part of the province? If the latter is true, the churches were founded on the first missionary journey (Ac 13:3—14:26). If the former is true, it is argued that missionary activity in the area was carried on during the second missionary journey, as indicated in Acts 18:23.

While the Galatian epistle certainly could speak to Christians of the whole province of Galatia, it seems to be intended primarily for those of the southern cities where Barnabas and Paul went on their first missionary journey. There is no specific account of churches having been founded in North Galatia, even on the second missionary journey, and there is no certainty that churches existed there this early. When the collection for the Jerusalem poor was sent to Palestine, two representatives of South Galatia accompanied the gift (Gaius of Derbe and Timothy, Ac 20:4) but no representatives of North Galatian churches are mentioned. Moreover, South Galatia would have been more accessible to the Judaizers than the northern churches; and Barnabas (Gal 2:13) would not have been personally known to northern believers, because he accompanied Paul only on the first journey.

Paul, proud of his Roman citizenship, always used the provincial names of the areas under Roman control, never the territorial, except as the two were identical in significance. Paul used the term *Galatia* only three times: in 1 Corinthians 16:1; Galatians 1:2; and 2 Timothy 4:10—all of which certainly must refer to the Roman province. Peter must have used the term in the same sense in 1 Peter 1:1, because the other four areas he addressed in the same verse were adjacent Roman provinces.

Now what of Luke's use of the term *Galatia*? Did Paul even visit North Galatia? Luke does not use either "Galatia" or "Galatians" but only the adjective "Galatic" or "Galatian." Following Ramsay, Souter argues that Acts 16:6 should be translated "the Phrygo-Galatic region," which no doubt referred to that section of the province of Galatia known as Phrygia Galatica, containing Pisidian Antioch and Iconium. He further argues that in Acts 18:23 the Greek may be translated either "the Galatico-Phrygian region" or "the Galatian region and Phrygia" (preferably the latter), the Galatian region including Derbe and Lystra, and the Phrygian, Iconium and Pisidian Antioch.[2]

Ramsay also notes that Acts 16:6 must be looked upon as connected with Acts 15:36 and 16:1-2, verses 3 to 5 being considered as somewhat parenthetical.[3] According to this passage, the apostle purposed to visit churches he had previously founded in Derbe, Lystra, Iconium, and Antioch.

After he had visited these towns, Luke said, "When they had gone throughout the Phrygo-Galatic region . . ." (Ac 16:6), indicating that those four towns were in Galatia. Obviously there is no room here for the idea that Paul on this journey circled far north through the old ethnic area of Galatia. This writer does not feel there is much support for the north Galatian theory, in regard to Paul's either having visited the area or writing his epistle to the people of it. Acts 18:23 marks the beginning of Paul's third missionary journey and refers to the fact that he went through the Galatic region and Phrygia, strengthening the disciples. The obvious implication would seem to be that he visited the churches he had founded on his first journey at Derbe, Lystra, Iconium, and Antioch and had again ministered to on his second journey. There is no certain proof that the apostle ever visited the northern part of the province.

TIME AND PLACE OF WRITING

If it may be assumed that Paul addressed churches in the chief towns of the southern part of Galatia, it may next be asked when he wrote the epistle and from where. The last phrase of Galatians 4:13 is generally thought to be properly translated "the first time" and to imply that a second visit had been made to these people. If so, the second visit may apply to the apostle's second visit on the first missionary journey, because he returned to all of the south Galatian towns on his way back to Antioch. The epistle could then have been written as early as A.D. 48, before the Council of Jerusalem (Ac 15), and thus be the earliest of Paul's epistles. This date is attractive because it would put the confrontation between Paul and Peter

(Gal 2:11-14) before the Council of Jerusalem. The place of writing would then probably be at Antioch. More commonly, however, Paul's second visit to the Galatians is interpreted as occurring on the second missionary journey. Therefore composition may have occurred at Corinth during the second journey (about 52) or while he was at Ephesus on the third journey—too busy to leave his work to deal with the error of legalism. If Paul wrote from Ephesus, perhaps it was during 55 or 56. In any case, the date and place of composition are not certain and there is not space here to discuss all facets of the arguments for determining the exactness of either.

PURPOSE OF WRITING

Disturbing news reached the apostle from Galatia. False teachers had visited the churches, preaching that Christ's work on the cross was insufficient for salvation and had to be supplemented by keeping the Mosaic law, which was of divine origin. Their tactics were to cast doubt on Paul's message by questioning his apostleship, to glorify various aspects of Judaism, and to portray liberty in Christ as leading to a life of lawlessness or license. By way of attack, Paul had first to vindicate his apostleship, his right to speak. Then he had to defend his doctrine of justification by faith in Christ alone. Finally he had to show that the life of Christian liberty does not mean a life of license. If a Christian is properly related to Christ, he lives by the power of the Holy Spirit. The fruit of such a life is good works. In a word, the purpose of the epistle is to steer the Galatian Christians from the error of Judaism back into the path of liberty in Christ. The six chapters of the book rather easily divide into three pairs: the first two vindicate Paul's apostleship, the second two vindicate his message of justification by faith, and the last two vindicate the life of Christian liberty.

OUTLINE

Greetings, 1:1-5

The Occasion: Defection from Christian Liberty, 1:6-9

I. Paul's Defense of His Right to Preach Christian Liberty, 1:10—2:21
   A. His apostleship based on divine intervention in his life, 1:10-17
   B. His apostleship not dependent on the Jerusalem church, 1:18-24
   C. His apostleship confirmed by the Jerusalem church, 2:1-10
   D. His apostleship steadfast before erring Peter, 2:11-21

II. Justification by Faith as the Basis of Christian Liberty, 3:1—4:31
   A. Justification evidenced in initial experience of Galatians, 3:1-5
   B. Justification experienced by Abraham, 3:6-9
   C. Deliverance from law-works through Christ, 3:10-14
   D. Inability of law to alter the covenant with Abraham, 3:15-18
   E. True place and purpose of the law, 3:19-29
   F. Contrasted position under law and faith, 4:1-7

1

GREETINGS
1:1-5

This letter to a young church (to borrow an idea from J. B. Phillips) follows the customary pattern of letters written during the first century. In these communications, the writer names himself and his addressee, sends a greeting, and then launches into the main body of the letter with its statement of the business at hand. Although greetings are in order toward the end of a first-century letter, they are not always included. Paul does not extend them in Galatians, though he does in other letters.

Whether Paul's writings should be classified as letters or epistles is a question of more than academic interest. Though the two are similar in form, the epistle is usually described as a conscious literary effort designed for publication, whereas a letter is private in character (whether written to an individual or group), is destined to meet a specific need, and is not designed for posterity. While most of Paul's writings clearly bear more of the characteristics of a letter than an epistle, their literary elements should not be ignored. Moreover, although the apostle possibly did not consciously write for posterity, the Holy

Spirit obviously meant that his writings should have a continuing relevance. In fact, Paul in some instances intended that his message be circulated beyond its original circle of readers (see, e. g., Col 4:16).

From the very first verse of Galatians it is clear that this letter is quite different in tone from Paul's other writings. There is nothing unusual about the name Paul, the apostle's Gentile name, because it is always used of him in connection with his Gentile work. Nor is there anything unusual about the fact that he calls himself an apostle, because he does also in six other salutations (1 Co, 2 Co, Eph, Col, 1 Ti, 2 Ti). But in the Galatian churches, agitators had challenged the author's right to the title of apostle—his right to speak authoritatively. Thus Paul is more self-consciously on the offensive than in any of his other epistles. Immediately he seeks to make clear the divine source of his apostleship.

"Envoy" is perhaps the best translation of *apostle* (Gk, *apostolos*), though "delegate," "messenger," or "ambassador" are other valid translations in various contexts (e.g., "messenger" in Phil 2:25; 2 Co 8:23). Even before Jesus applied this descriptive term to the Twelve it apparently had attained a certain official connotation among the Jews. It referred to an envoy accredited by some authority and entrusted with a special message. This usage continued through the first century in Jewish-Christian circles, as is evident from the *Didache,* or *Teaching of the Twelve,* a church manual composed early in the second century.

If these troublemakers who sought to destroy the ministry of the gospel in Galatia claimed authority as envoys of the mother church in Jerusalem (Gal 2:12), Paul would

meet them head on. His commission came not from men.
Probably he meant to imply that his apostolic commission
was not from the Twelve. Or he may have meant that it
did not come from the church of Antioch (Ac 13:1-3),
which some may have thought to be inferior to a Jerusalem commission. Moreover, his commission came not
through or by means of man. The shift from the plural to
the singular apparently occurs to parallel with the reference to Jesus Christ. This shift tends to confirm Paul's belief in Christ as divine, because he declares that his apostolic authority comes not from *man* but Jesus Christ. The
commission came by or through the mediation of Jesus
Christ from God the Father. In making such a claim, no
doubt Paul had in mind his direct confrontation with the
risen Christ on the Damascus Road. The emphasis on the
resurrection of Christ in the last clause of verse 1 certainly reflects the tremendous impression made on Paul
by the sudden realization while on the Damascus Road
that Jesus really had risen from the dead (Ac 9:4-6).
Paul's apostleship or position as an envoy was then superior to any commission that the Judaizers may have received, for it came directly from the Father through His
risen and glorified Son.

After a parenthetical statement on the source of his
apostleship, Paul stops to associate the brethren with him
in sending greetings (1:2). Normally Paul singled out
individuals who were joining him in such pleasantries
(e.g., 1 Co 1:1; Col 1:1). Here he may have avoided the
practice because no one known to them was present. Or
possibly he wished in this way to insure a greater independence of message and apostleship—these came from

God. He was dependent on no man, neither apostles nor
fellow workers.   Even if Galatian Christians were present
at the time it may not have been wise to name them because their home churches (now steeped in legalism)
might have repudiated their message and friendship.
"The brethren . . . with me" does not seem to refer to a
church, as some have supposed, because he never associates a church with himself in any of his other epistles.
Probably these are simply his special friends and workers
with him at the time. *Brethren* (*adelphoi*) as a term
signifying religious relationship was applied to religious
associations at least as early as the second century B.C.
But it was given a new depth and beauty by Christians.
Christian brethren are individuals who enjoy a common
bond because they have become members of the household of faith on the basis of the finished work of Christ.

The addressees of the epistle are the "churches of Galatia." As already noted in the Introduction, these were
probably located in Derbe, Lystra, Iconium, and Antioch
of Pisidia. Possibly this is the only time Paul addressed a
group of churches, although the Ephesian* letter may
also have been a circular letter to churches of the western
part of the province of Asia Minor.

Church (Gk, *ekklēsia*) is a beautiful word. It means
"called-out ones" and in the New Testament context refers
to individuals called out from a doomed and dying world
by the grace of God. Of course these called-out ones are

---

*"Ephesus" (Eph 1:1) does not appear in the best manuscripts and
some argue that a blank was left here in the original to be filled in by
each of the churches in the area. They argue further that the reason we
have "Ephesus" appearing in the New Testament book is that only the
Ephesian copy of this circular letter survived.

to remain in their society as salt and light to accomplish whatever purposes God has for them there. Paul used the term *church* to refer to an assembly gathered for worship (1 Co 14:28), a group of believers meeting in one house (Phile 2), believers of a town (Ro 16:1), and the whole body of believers everywhere (Col 1:18, 24).

Following proper epistolary form, the writer has identified himself and his addressees and now proceeds to pen a greeting, or salutation. "Grace be to you and peace" is the apostle's formula, appearing in all his letters to the churches. Some believe Paul coined this formula and others borrowed it from him. The common Greek greeting was *chairein,* "joy" to you. It is changed here to *charis,* meaning "grace" to you. "Peace" (Gk, *eirēnē*; Heb, *shalom*) is the Hebrew greeting. One would expect the apostle to the Gentiles to use a Greek greeting, especially when writing to churches of the Greek East. But he links the Greek with the Hebrew greeting, symbolizing the union of Jew and Greek in one body, the middle wall of partition having been broken down in Christ. Gentiles have now been admitted to privileges which had been peculiar to Israel. Grace always precedes peace in these salutations, for the free and unmerited favor of God must be extended before the individual can experience either peace with God or the peace of God. Findlay puts the relationship well:

> *Grace* is the sum of all blessing bestowed by God; *peace,* . . . the sum of all blessing experienced by man. *Grace* is the Father's good will and bounty in Christ to His undeserving children; *peace,* the rest and reconcilement, the recovered health and gladness of the child brought home

to the Father's house, dwelling in the light of his Father's
face. *Grace* is the fountain of redeeming love; *peace* is
the "river of life proceeding from the throne of God and
of the Lamb," that flows calm and deep through each believing soul, the river whose "streams make glad the city
of God."[1]

Grace and peace come from the Father and our Lord
Jesus Christ. The second *from* is not in the Greek and
should not be supplied. Grace and peace come from a
single divine source. The Father and Son cooperate in
closest union in preparing and carrying out the plan of
man's redemption. Nothing speaks more forcefully for the
deity of Christ than the way He is linked with the Father
here.

While the Father and the Son may have cooperated
fully in devising the plan of redemption, it was the Son
who "gave himself" unto death as an offering for our sins
(1:4). This is a statement of the true ground of acceptance before God. In turning to a system of salvation on
the basis of good works, the Galatians had practically
ignored the grace of God and the substitutionary death of
Christ (cf. 2:21; 5:4). Some New Testament passages
refer to Christ's giving Himself for sin and some refer to
His sacrifice for sinners. The former focus on the effect
of His work in dealing with sin and the latter on the mo-
tive for His sacrifice—love for sinners.

Christ gave Himself for our sins in order to "deliver us
from this present evil world." Our sins enslaved us and
Christ sought to pluck us out, or deliver us, as from bondage. The verb in the Greek suggests that He who delivers
us has an interest in the result of His act. Certainly de-

liverance would come through the work of Christ, not through human effort. "This present evil world [age]" refers to the corrupting influences of the world and its works. The phrase has been well translated "the present age with all its evils." This age is under a god (2 Co 4:4) or rulers (1 Co 2:6) of its own who are in opposition to the eternal God, the King of the ages (1 Ti 1:17; cf. Eph 2:2-7).

Christ's death on the cross was "according to the will of God." Jesus was fully conscious throughout His ministry that what He did was according to a divinely predetermined plan and He was subject to that plan. He predicted His death, burial, and resurrection on occasion. When in a dangerous spot He could know that His "time was not yet come." He is quoted as saying, "I come . . . to do thy will, O God" (Heb 10:7). After His prayer in the Garden of Gethsemane, He prayed, "Father, . . . take away this cup from me: nevertheless not what I will, but what thou wilt" (Mk 14:36).

"God and our Father." Salvation was provided by the sovereign God, who has by grace alone become our Father. We stand in filial relation to Him through no effort of our own. Thus the apostle paves the way for the main argument of the epistle. Next he breaks out in a paean of praise to such a wonderful God. "To whom be the glory," the glory which is exclusively His and which properly belongs to Him. This glory He will not share with men nor surrender to men who seek to gain their salvation in whole or in part by their own efforts. Throughout eternity He will solely be the object of praise by redeemed ones who testify that "salvation is of the LORD" (Jon 2:9).

2

THE OCCASION: DEFECTION FROM CHRISTIAN LIBERTY

1:6-9

Zealous for the glory of God, the apostle plunges immediately into a vehement denunciation of Galatian defection from Christian liberty to a legalistic stance. Since the Galatians were thus denying the grace of God and the message Paul preached, he omitted the usual extended thanksgiving for churches he had established and scored them instead for unfaithfulness to the truth.

"I marvel," or wonder (the verb frequently implies wondering at something blameworthy) "that ye are so soon removed from him." *Removed* is in the Greek present middle tense and should therefore be translated "you are in the process of removing yourselves." In other words, they were responsible for their own defection and the process was not yet complete. As the argument of the epistle progresses, however, the apostle makes it clear that the Galatians were not entirely to blame for their apostasy; false teachers (Judaizers) had come among them with their enticing message. "So soon" is variously

24

interpreted. If translated "so quickly" or "so soon," it may
apply to the short time that had elapsed after the arrival
of false teachers, or after the departure of Paul or after
their salvation before they turned away from the true
faith. Perhaps a better translation is "so readily." Possibly the apostle is accusing them of something akin to
fickleness: "I marvel that you are so readily shifting your
ground." The shift or removal was "from him that called
you." The one who calls in grace must be the Father, for
so He is commonly represented in the epistles (e.g., Gal
1:15; Eph 1:3-5). The assertion of turning from God may
have startled the Galatians. No doubt they thought they
were pleasing the Father by keeping the law, as did the
Jews and Paul before his conversion. But the Father now
calls in Christ's grace, the instrument by which, or the
element in which, He calls us to salvation.

"Another [Gk, *heteron*] gospel" (1:6) means another of
a different sort which has nothing in common with the
true gospel. In verse 7 the Greek word for "another" is
allo and means another of the same sort. So the gospel to
which the Galatians have turned is not at all of the same
sort as Paul preaches.

"Some that trouble you" is a deliberately vague descrip-
tion of Judaizers whom the apostle treats with contempt.
Apparently they were not Galatians but outsiders who
sought to *pervert* the gospel. The Greek has more the
sense of "to reverse." If they followed these teachers they
certainly would be taking a major step backward. It would
be a step in reverse to "turn . . . again to the weak and
beggarly elements" (Gal 4:9) or to think that having begun in the Spirit they could now be made perfect by the

flesh (Gal 3:3). Apparently what the Judaizers were teaching was the necessity of circumcision and keeping the law in order to achieve real Christian maturity on the part of those who were trusting in Christ. (See Ac 15:24, where *trouble* is the same Greek word as in Gal 1:7.)

Verse 8 really sets forth an impossibility that another gospel will be proclaimed. Paul and his companions will not do it; God has not ordained that angels should. In verse 7 Paul denied the existence of another gospel of the same sort as he has preached to the Galatians. Now he says that if anyone at all should preach to them a gospel other than (may be translated "contrary to" or "in addition to") what he has preached, *"let him be anathema."* "Anathema" is the Septuagint (Gk translation of the O. T.) rendering of Hebrew *cherem,* a thing devoted to God for preservation or destruction. While in some rabbinic and modern contexts it signifies simply excommunication, Paul uses it here as the strongest possible form of a curse. Just as Paul called down a curse on any who added to the requirements of the gospel, so John hurled a curse at those who added or subtracted from the message of Revelation (see Rev 22:18-19).

On the face of it, verse 9 seems to be largely a repetition of the curse enunciated in verse 8. But there are important differences. In verse 8 the subjunctive is used— "should preach." In verse 9 the Greek suggests that at least one person is actually preaching this false gospel. Another difference is that in verse 9 Paul observes, "As we said before." This is too emphatic to refer to the previous verse and is assumed to refer to the apostle's last visit among them. At that time he felt the need of warning them against possible false teaching which apparently had not yet actually come among them. Moreover, while verse 8 refers to Paul's preaching among them, verse 9 alludes to their reception of his message. So this verse is really quite strong language. It recalls the apostle's warning in person of impending apostasy, alludes to an actual outbreak of heretical teaching among them, reminds them of their genuine reception of the truth at his hands, and pronounces a curse on the false teachers who are subverting them.

3

PAUL'S DEFENSE OF HIS RIGHT TO PREACH CHRISTIAN LIBERTY

1:10—2:21

His Apostleship Based on Divine Intervention in His Life (1:10-17)

Paul now moves into the next major section of the epistle, in which he defends his right to preach the gospel of grace and Christian liberty. He must clearly vindicate his apostleship before he can vindicate his message. Immediately he is on the defensive: "Am I now persuading men rather than God?" (1:10). Probably he was accused of sacrificing the truth of God or of softening truths unwelcome to men so he might win them over to his way of thinking. This would apply especially to dropping the requirement of keeping the law by Gentile believers in an effort to gain their support—accommodating the gospel to the heathen. Paul admits that there was a time when he sought to please men ("if I yet pleased men") before his conversion. But now "I should not be Christ's slave if I yet pleased men." If he pleased men he would still curry favor with the Jews by persecuting Christians. He would

28

be cutting corners doctrinally to avoid persecution. In reality he was concerned with pleasing God only. He has already made it clear in this epistle that salvation is by grace alone and one can enjoy true Christian liberty—freed from this present evil world—by the power of Christ alone. As was to be very clear from Paul's experience, preaching of that sort would not please men and would not lead to an easy life for him. Rather, the way would be very difficult, involving much physical suffering and even death.

"I certify," (1:11) or make known (Gk, *gnōrizō*), appears only in the nearly contemporary Corinthian letters (1 Co 12:3; 15:1; 2 Co 8:1) and introduces in each case subjects of great importance. Paul addresses the "brethren" nine times in this epistle, signifying not only their position in Christ but his personal acquaintance with them. He was no stranger to them. He had preached among them and they had received him and his gospel. "Gospel" sometimes refers to basic historical facts such as the death, burial, and resurrection of Christ and sometimes to the interpretation and application of those facts in terms of salvation by faith and the like. The latter must be true here, for Judaizers would accept the former but hedge on aspects of the application of the work of Christ to mankind. Paul insists that his statement of the gospel is not "after man" (1:11) or according to man, either in nature or authority. It is not measured by merely human rules but is above man's devising. If man were responsible for the plan of salvation, he would inject a large dose of human works. He cannot on the one hand conceive of salvation being granted by the grace of God alone, and he

does not on the other hand want a humiliating arrangement in which he cannot get credit for having made it
largely on his own. Man wants credit for his efforts.

The apostle now advances his thought another step.
Not only is his message above man's devising, but he did
not receive it from man as an intermediate source; that is,
he had not learned it from human teaching as his converts
had. Neither was he taught it by man; the labor of learning was absent. But he "received it by revelation of Jesus
Christ." Paul obtained his message by direct revelation
from Jesus Christ as the Twelve had learned at His feet
(cf. Mt 16:17). This revelation apparently began with the
vision on the Damascus Road and continued during the
three years of seclusion in Arabia (Gal 1:17-18).

In verses 13 and 14 the apostle makes it clear that there
was no preparation for his present life in the life he lived
before his conversion. Certainly his present message could
not have originated in his previous way of life. "You have
heard," probably from Paul's own lips or those of his
friends when evangelizing among them, "of my former
conversation [way of life] in times past in *Judaism.*" *Iou-
daisma* indicates all that is peculiar to Judaism. It refers
to the government, laws, institutions, and religion of the
Jews. There is nothing particularly disparaging in the
term. Then the apostle goes on to show why his former
life could not be a preparation for present ministry by way
of a declaration of what he used to do. "Persecuted,"
"wasted," and "profited" are all in the Greek imperfect
tense, indicating the long continuance of this mode of life.
He kept on earnestly pursuing the church and kept on
wasting it. Violent in his opposition to believers in Jeru-

salem (9:13), he was even responsible for the death of some (26:11). But his persecuting efforts extended to other towns besides Jerusalem, and Paul was on the way to Damascus to persecute believers there when God met him and changed his whole pattern of life (26:12-18).

Since Saul, a very devout Jew, was involved in violent persecution of the *church*, it is clear that Jews of the New Testament period were not by natural birth members of the church. It is true that Jews in the Sinai wilderness under Moses' leadership were referred to as an *ekklēsia*— a people "called out" from among the nations as a testimony to God (Ac 7:38). But the New Testament church as a body of believers must be regarded as a fellowship distinct from Jews and Gentiles (see 1 Co 10:32). In his zeal Paul "profited," or rather kept on striking forward, in Judaism. Striking forward (*prokoptō*) may at times have an evil or a good connotation, but here it seems to be used in a neutral sense. Saul advanced in Judaism beyond many of his equals or of his own age, showing great zeal for the traditions of his fathers. "Traditions of my fathers" here refers not to the national law and customs of Israel but to the oral law or traditions, especially as held by the Pharisees. Saul's family held membership in one of the strictest of the Pharisaical sects.

While Saul struck forward in Judaism, enjoying great success and prestige, God had other plans for him. *But*— the contrast is between the former life of Saul and what is going to take place after God's intervention. God "separated" (1:15) ("to mark off from") him from the womb, even before Saul could exercise independent willpower.

In commenting on this sovereign act of God, Rendall beautifully observes:

> Paul looks back on his parentage and early years as a providential preparation for his future ministry: this view is justified by his antecedents. By birth at once a Hebrew, a Greek and Roman citizen, educated in the Hebrew Scriptures and in Greek learning, he combined in his own person the most essential requisite for an Apostle to the Gentiles. He was further moulded by the spiritual discipline of an intense, though mistaken, zeal for the Law of his God, which issued in bitter remorse. By this career he was fitted to become a chosen vessel to bear the name of Christ before the Gentile world. He did not hesitate accordingly to regard himself like Hebrew prophets of old as dedicated from his birth to the service of God.[1]

"Called" is in the aorist tense, which indicates an action at a point of time in the past. It refers to the apostle's conversion experience on the Damascus Road (cf. Ac 9:1-9). By His good pleasure, God marked Saul off for distinctive service and by His grace He efficaciously called the young Pharisee on the Damascus Road to a new life in Christ.

The last clause of verse 15 belongs with the first half of verse 16. God's call was to eventuate in Paul's effective ministry among the Gentiles. But this outpouring of spiritual blessing was impossible apart from a spiritual intake. "To reveal his Son in me" (v. 16) is variously understood by the commentators, but it seems clear that the general tenor of the passage involves getting the message to transmit it. The Son must be revealed in the innermost being by the Holy Spirit so the Son may be revealed through the apostle to the Gentiles. The revelation to Saul occurred on the Damascus Road and was enlarged upon during subsequent days in Damascus and Arabia. Note that Paul was to preach Christ among the Gentiles; no reference is made to Mosaic law or ceremonialism or anything else being added to the gospel. "I conferred not" underscores the fact that Paul's message did not come from men but by revelation from God. "Confer" here is "to lay any matter before others with a view to obtaining advice or instruction." "Flesh and blood" refers to the limitations or weaknesses of men. Weak men could not add much to a divine revelation.

"Neither" (lit., not even) did Paul go to Jerusalem after his conversion to confer with the apostles (1:17). Although he did not choose to consult with others, he might have been expected to confer with the apostles; but such was not the case. To go "up to Jerusalem" would often be necessary from a geographical point of view, for the city is over twenty-five hundred feet in altitude and is therefore higher than many other places in Palestine. In addition, its religious significance as seat of the temple and mother church elevated the city in the thinking of most people so they normally spoke of going up to Jerusalem.

An apostle is one sent or commissioned to preach the gospel. The term applies especially to the Twelve, which came to include Matthias after the defection and death of Judas, and possibly may have included James. Although Paul and Barnabas (1 Co 9:1-2; Ac 14:14) and others (Ro 16:7) could be so designated, the reference here concerns Jerusalem and therefore must be used in a restrictive sense.

After his conversion on the Damascus Road Paul did not seek out anyone to confer about the gospel but went out to Arabia. Arabia was divided into three sections at this point in history. Reference in Galatians must be to Arabia Petraea, the northwest section of Arabia, controlled by the Nabataeans. Their kingdom stretched from the Sinai north to Syria. Aretas IV ruled from 9 B.C. to A.D. 40. Damascus was actually under the rule of a governor appointed by Aretas when Paul fled the city (2 Co 11:32). The demands of the Galatians narrative are completely satisfied with a view that Paul went out into the region around Damascus during this period of time and then subsequently returned to Damascus. There is no evidence, indeed no likelihood, that he ranged as far south as Mount Sinai at this time. Nor is there any evidence that he went about preaching in Syrian villages as if on an evangelistic tour. His purpose in going was to enjoy uninterrupted communion with God in a learning experience. After such a time he would be ready to preach.

His Apostleship Not Dependent on the Jerusalem Church (1:18-24)

In this section we note that Paul saw only two of the apostles after his sojourn in Arabia and then only for a short time. Furthermore, they recognized his ministry. "Then" (*epeita*) appears in 1:18, 1:21 (translated "afterwards"), and 2:1 to introduce three events in the apostle's contact with the Jerusalem church: his introduction to them, his departure for ministry, and his return to Jerusalem with Barnabas. "After three years." In an effort to underscore his independence of the Jerusalem church, Paul observes that three full years elapsed between his conversion and any significant contact with them. When he finally went up to see Peter, it was not for the purpose of learning the gospel. The significance of the word *see* here is "to visit with a view to becoming acquainted with." He only remained in Jerusalem for fifteen days, not long enough to learn extensively of the gospel or to become Peter's disciple. This visit of Paul to Jerusalem is commonly taken to be the one recorded in Acts 9:26-29. Suddenly driven from his ministry in Damascus, the apostle apparently sought to determine where to go next. Possibly he sought the advice of Peter concerning a future course of action.

A reason why Paul did not see more of the apostles (1:19) may be that they were away at the time. *Other* is not to be understood in the qualitative but the numerical sense. James, though not one of the Twelve, was a pillar of the church at Jerusalem and an apostle in the wider sense (cf. Ac 14:14). James as *brother* of the Lord is variously understood. Some argue that he was the son of Joseph by a previous marriage, others that he was a cousin, and yet others that he was a younger son of Joseph and Mary. The latter seems preferable.

In verse 20 the apostle calls the Galatians to witness that he is telling the truth. The nature of the appeal shows the intensity of his desire either to maintain independence of human teachers or to answer malicious attacks hurled against him. Probably both were necessary.

Apparently at the end of Paul's fifteen-day visit to Jerusalem (1:18) some Jews who had been imbued with rationalistic Hellenistic ways ("Grecians," Ac 9:29) concocted a plot against him. When the brethren found out about it, they brought him down to the seaport of Caesa-

rea and sent him off to Tarsus, his home city (Ac 9:30).
"Afterwards" (Gal 1:21), the apostle went to Syria and Cilicia where he preached the faith (v. 23). Probably the order in which the two provinces appear here is not intended
to describe the order in which Paul visited them. In sail-
ing from Caesarea to Tarsus, he would have gone first to
Cilicia, of which Tarsus was the chief city. In Paul's day
Cilicia and Syria were joined for administrative purposes,
and the latter with its great city of Antioch and other major centers was more important in terms of wealth and
population than the former. So Syria appears first here because of its greater prominence. What Paul did in those
early years at Tarsus we are left to conjecture. But apparently he was in the process of establishing a Christian testimony. This seems evident from the fact that when church
growth at Antioch required additional and effective leadership, Barnabas brought Paul from Tarsus to Antioch.
There Paul labored successfully for a year or more (Ac 11:
24-26).

Since Paul had carried on his ministry for a decade or
more at such a great distance from Jerusalem, he was obviously independent of the mother church. In fact, he was
even "unknown by face unto the churches of Judaea" (v.
22). A better translation of the Greek is "becoming unknown." Certainly at the time of his conversion Paul was
quite familiar to persecuted Christians; but with an ab-
sence of more than ten years a new generation was rising
that did not know him. Possibly this verse intends to dis-
tinguish between churches of Judea and Jerusalem. Certainly most brethren of Judea would not have known him,
although he had returned to Jerusalem for fifteen days

(Gal 1:18) and had made another secret visit to Jerusalem during his fruitful Antioch ministry to bring a gift from the Antioch church to the Jerusalem church (Ac 11:29-30). While he may have come to know some of the brethren on the latter occasion, he would not have visited with any of the apostles or learned at their feet. A great persecution was in progress; many were scattered, James was martyred, and Peter was in prison. Hence it did not seem to be germane to Paul's argument even to mention this hurried and secret visit.

The brethren of Judea did not know Paul personally but "had heard only" (lit., "were hearing" from time to time), reports of his magnificent about-face and ministry (1:23). He was now preaching *the faith*, which has become a synonym for "the gospel." There is a clear implication in *the faith* to a salvation available by faith alone rather than by human effort. While faith is made to stand for gospel, it is also made to stand for those who hold it. Faith was enshrined in the hearts of men, and apparently there was a day when Paul thought he could destroy the Christian faith by destroying those who held it. That may well have seemed practicable to opponents of Christianity when the movement was small, but the sovereign power of God would not permit such obliteration.

When the churches of Judea (including Jerusalem) heard of Paul's preaching of the faith, "they glorified God." *Glorified* is in the Greek imperfect tense, which denotes continuous action. They kept on glorifying, not the one who was preaching but the one who had brought about the change in him. In respect to "in me," Hogg and Vine observe,

These words mark a climax in the Apostle's argument; the
Christians in Judaea had praised God for the preaching
of the very same gospel with which those who professed
to come from Judaea found fault as inadequate.[2]

HIS APOSTLESHIP CONFIRMED BY THE JERUSALEM
CHURCH (2:1-10)

In previous verses Paul has been careful to underscore
the divine origin of his message and his independence
from the apostolic company, the churches of Judea, and
Christian brethren elsewhere. Paul might successfully es-
tablish himself as a loner. Could he also win the full approval of the apostles and the mother church? Could he
prove that his ministry and message flowed in the main-
stream of Christianity? This fact he now sets about to
demonstrate.

It is clear from previous verses that Paul's contacts with
the apostles since his conversion had been few and brief.
Now finally "fourteen years after" (2:1), he has some sort
of official confrontation with church leaders in Jerusalem.
One might conclude that the fourteen years date from the
last major event referred to in the epistle—his journey to
Syria and Cilicia—which was at least three years after his
conversion. Many argue, however, that the fourteen years
must date from Paul's conversion because there is not
room in the chronology to date it from the later event.

The time of this visit to Jerusalem is also problematical;
it may refer to the famine-relief visit of Acts 9:30 or the
theological debate recorded in Acts 15. Possibly the latter
is preferable. Both in Galatians 2 and Acts 15 the issue of
law-keeping or liberty is central, and both Barnabas and

Paul are in Jerusalem to try to hammer out a settlement
with church leaders. Titus is probably mentioned in 2:1
because of the issue which he at the same time represented
and occasioned. He was an uncircumcised Gentile Christian. Should he be forced to submit to circumcision as part
of the legal obligation of *all* Christians? (see Ac 15:1-6).
If Galatians was written after the great Council of Jerusalem (A.D. 49 or 50; Ac 15:1-6) when it was decided that
law-keeping was not necessary for Gentiles, one might expect Paul to have referred to the council decision here.
But that decision was not germane to his controversy with
the Galatians. They apparently believed that while law-
keeping was not necessary, it brought a higher perfection
(3:3). And Paul's contention was that law-keeping was
not only not necessary but was now at an end and could
add nothing to the perfect work of Christ.

As Paul went to Jerusalem to deal with the question of
law-keeping, he asserts he went up "by revelation" (2:2).
Possibly this revelation came first to Paul and he then
prompted the church to action, or possibly it came to the
church corporately and thus to Paul as a member of the
church. At any rate, clearly God did the appointing; and
he (Paul) was not under human authority. Believers in
Antioch concurred in commissioning Paul and Barnabas
to go to Jerusalem to thresh out the matter (Ac 15:2). He
"communicated unto them," or "laid before them," or "related with a view to consulting." *Them* refers to members
of the church at Jerusalem. Paul and Barnabas and their
companions followed two courses of action. They spoke to
the mother church in a general way in public addresses
and to the leaders privately and in greater detail concern-

ing the gospel Paul had been preaching among the Gentiles. This *gospel* or good news concerned salvation by grace through faith alone. *Preach* is in the present tense and shows that Paul had not ceased to preach this gospel but was continuing to preach it. "Those of reputation" is not a descriptive of disrepute but one of honor. It indicates that they are of repute among men and does not imply that they seem to be something they are not. Paul must convince the church leaders and through them the Judean church of the validity of his position that Gentiles were not under law. If he failed to do so, he would "run in vain." His past work, as well as present and future work, would be hindered or even rendered of no effect if now law-keeping was necessary to perfect the work of Christ.

The apostle had resisted all Judaizing pressures upon him to circumcise Titus and thus capitulate to the principle of law-keeping. Titus was a Greek, a full-blooded Gentile. Therefore no special circumstances need be brought to bear as in the case of Timothy. The latter was half Jew and circumcising him alleviated difficulties in some circles (Ac 16:3).

Verses 4 and 5 explain why, as a matter of principle, Paul did not agree to the circumcision of Titus. He could not possibly succumb to such a proposal when advanced by false teachers. *False brethren,* misbelievers who added law-keeping to belief in Christ, had been brought in secretly—probably by overzealous law keepers. These individuals were brought in secretly or surreptitiously, by whom we do not know. These false brethren stole in like spies to search out weak points in an enemy position. In this case they sought to overturn the *liberty,* or "unfettered

condition of the Christian soul," and bring believers back
into bondage. These false brethren may have posed as
representatives of the Jerusalem church as they stirred up
trouble in Antioch, but the Jerusalem church repudiated
any official connection with these individuals (Ac 15:24).
To these false teachers Paul and Barnabas (we, 2:5) did
not yield "by subjection" even for a moment. If no principle were involved they might have yielded in love, but
they would not do so in subjection to law or legalizers.
Their momentary yielding in the circumcision of Titus
might have quieted the Judaizers briefly, but the issue at
stake now would not have been resolved and the gospel
would have been perverted. Paul was determined that
the truth of the gospel be preserved "for you," namely,
for your welfare.

After a parenthetical statement about Titus in verses
3-5, Paul returns to the subject he was discussing in verse
2. In Jerusalem he conferred privately with those "who
seemed to be somewhat," or those "reputed to be something." Here Paul takes the term used by the Judaizers
for James and the Twelve, whom they pitted against Paul.
Parenthetically Paul says the greatness of their reputation
really didn't matter to him—his gospel came from God
Himself. But he hastens to add that God accepts no man's
person, not even Paul's. Thus the apostle makes it clear
that neither the Twelve nor he nor anyone else really
makes any special impression on God. Moreover, the message of no Christian worker is superior or right because of
the greatness of the worker.

After the parenthesis Paul again refers to those who
"seemed to be somewhat." It should be clear from the

context that Paul does not mean to degrade the position
or reputation of the Jerusalem leadership. The respect he
accorded them is evident from the very fact he comes to
them for a definitive solution to a knotty problem. One
would expect the "top brass" to correct Paul in some way,
but he startlingly announces, "they placed nothing before
me" (KJV, "added nothing to me").

Quite the opposite of finding fault with Paul's ministry,
James, Cephas, and John recognized that Paul had been
made an apostle to the Gentiles as Peter had been to the
Jews. The distinction seems to be more geographical than
ethnographical. Peter ministered primarily in Palestine
(including Gentiles there; e.g., Cornelius); Paul ministered primarily in Gentile territory (but always went to
the Jews first in territory visited). Moreover, the apostles
recognized that Paul had not launched into a ministry to
Gentiles on his own; it was a stewardship entrusted (1 Co
9:17). What brought the apostles to the conclusion that
Paul had a commission or apostleship equal to Peter's was
the fact that God had wrought just as great spiritual works
through the former as the latter (v. 8).

James, Cephas, and John are the subjects in verses 6-10.
Now (2:9) they are specifically named. The fact that
James (a strict legalist) appears first gives special significance to the decision concerning Gentile freedom. He had
become head of the Jerusalem church. While it was necessary to identify the James meant in Galatians 1:19, James
the son of Zebedee had been put to death between the
two Jerusalem visits of 1:19 and 2:1. This James is clearly "our Lord's brother." Peter commonly went by his Hebrew surname, Cephas, in Jerusalem. These men "seemed,"

that is, "were reputed," to be strong or powerful supporters
of the church. Now these great leaders who saw that Paul
had been made apostle to the Gentiles (v. 7) and per-
ceived (v. 9) or understood the full significance of that
fact, gave Paul and Barnabas the right hand of fellowship.
The church leaders came to a full understanding with Paul
and Barnabas and gave their full blessing to them. There
was no effort to upbraid them or set them straight. They
only requested the missionary pair to remember the poor—
Jewish Christians in Judea. These brethren were in chronic
poverty, partly because of social and religious persecution
and partly because of the generally low economy of the
area. Paul was "forward" or zealous to provide this help
(1 Co 16:1-3; 2 Co 9:1 ff.; Ro 15:26-27; Ac 24:17). Barnabas is not mentioned in connection with this provision
because he did not accompany Paul after the first journey.

His Apostleship Steadfast Before Erring Peter
(2:11-21)

After the Jerusalem Council Paul and Barnabas returned
to Antioch. Great rejoicing occurred there over the council
decision, which was worded as follows: "We trouble not
them, which from among the Gentiles are turned to God:
but that we write unto them that they abstain from pollu-
tions of idols, and from fornication, and from things stran-
gled, and from blood" (Ac 15:19-20). In other words
Gentiles were not under the law but were expected to
avoid certain pagan religious and social practices for the
sake of the Christian testimony. For a while all went well
in Antioch. Such great love sprang up between Jewish
and Gentile believers that they ate the agapē, or love-

feast, together. This practice was an emblem of Christian unity and the interruption of it was sure to harm the church. An outbreak of factionalism, contributed to by Peter, therefore drew fire from Paul. No such disturbance could be permitted, especially when it threatened Christian liberty. Acts 15 records no visit of Peter to Antioch and the altercation to which Paul refers in Galatians 2: 11-14. Some have accounted for this omission on the basis of its transitory nature; it had no permanent effect on church history.

When Peter became involved in this breach of fellowship, Paul opposed him openly. A private conference might have changed Peter's course of action, but it would not clearly enunciate the principle of Christian liberty. Peter was condemned (Gk) not by observers but by the act itself. When Peter first came to Antioch he ate with Gentiles, probably even partaking of the love-feast with them. But when some came "from James" (2:12) the situation changed radically. It is difficult to know how to understand "from James." That these men came from the Jerusalem church of which James was leader is undisputed. James may even have sent them, but certainly not with a special message concerning doctrine or practice so soon after his dictum issued by the Jerusalem council. Possibly he sent out a group to raise funds for the poor. If this was an official delegation, they may have expressed on the side James' personal view that Jewish Christians should keep the law, even if Gentiles did not. Or they may simply have expressed their own view on the subject. At any rate, as a result of a visit by Jews from the Jerusalem church, pressure was exerted on Jews at Antioch not to eat with

Gentiles and to be more scrupulous about law-keeping. Peter, who had taken such a forceful stand for Jewish fellowship with Gentiles (Ac 11:1-18), buckled under social pressure—"fearing them which were of the circumcision." He "began to withdraw" and finally "separated himself" in a complete severance.

When Peter capitulated, other Jews found it hard to stand against the tide. They "dissembled" also (v. 13), that is, pretended to follow a course of action for one reason when they actually did so for another reason. In other words, they withdrew more out of fear of Judaizers than loyalty to Moses. Even Barnabas ultimately fell before the social pressure. This is hard to believe, because his home (Cyprus) was a Gentile center, he had had widespread ministry among Gentiles, and he was now ministering in a large Gentile Christian stronghold. The pressure must have been enormous. Of course it was also true that Barnabas was a member of the Jerusalem church (Ac 4:36-37; 9:26-27) and their delegate to Antioch (Ac 11:22); thus there could have been pressure on him in that connection.

Observing that the Judaizers did not walk uprightly (viz., "deal straightforwardly") in accordance with the gospel in casting a slur of uncleanness on those cleansed in Christ, Paul launched a frontal attack on this error. He took Peter to task "before them all," probably the whole church. Verse 15 should read parenthetically in apposition to "thou" of verse 14: "If thou—we who are born Jews (not Jews by proselytism) and not open sinners from among the Gentiles (i.e., without law and without the moral restraints of Judaism)—" The sense of verse 14 seems to be: If you, a born Jew, live like a Gentile (as if not under law and certainly not as if law can justify), why do you now by example compel Gentiles to live as Jews (and adopt dietary laws and circumcision)? Obligation to law-keeping would not be "according to the truth of the gospel" or the pronouncements of the Council of Jerusalem.

In fact, no one can be justified "by the works of the law" (v. 16). Law was a standard of conduct so exacting that no one ever kept it wholly; therefore all the law could do was condemn (cf. Ro 3:20). Justification, being declared righteous in God's eyes and released from any condemnation involved in failure to keep God's law, comes "by the faith of Jesus Christ"—faith in Christ as the ground of justification (cf. Ro 3:21-24).

Verse 17 is very difficult to interpret and numerous views have been given. One that seems to fit the tenor of the verse and the context goes like this: If we seek to be justified by Christ alone and no longer put ourselves under the restraints of the law, perhaps we are in this way giving license to sin. If free grace in Christ encourages men to continue in sin, then He is made a minister of sin. Paul finds such a view utterly repulsive and retorts with his characteristic "God forbid" ("perish the thought").

"If I build again the things which I destroyed" (v. 18) involves restoring to the believer the whole system of legal righteousness overthrown by the faith of Christ. Though Paul uses the first person, he is clearly referring to Peter. If he restored the law, Peter would be a transgressor or sinner in the sight of the law, because he had set it aside and lived as a Gentile; therefore he could not be justified by the law. He would also be a transgressor in the light of the true gospel because in reestablishing the system of legal righteousness he would deny the sufficiency of justification by faith in Christ alone.

Some argue that verse 19 simply describes how Paul came to the end of himself and turned to God for justification. They say Paul finally became exhausted in his zeal for keeping the law. The condemnation the law administered drove him to Christ for deliverance from his spiritual predicament. Thus through the law he really died to it in that being joined to Christ freed him from the law and enables him to live on an entirely new plane spiritually.

All this may be true but it seems to make much more sense to link verse 19 to verse 20 and to pursue a somewhat different doctrinal emphasis. All the law could do was condemn. Its standard of ethical and moral righteousness was so demanding that no mere human being could fulfill it. The law demanded death for lawbreakers; so all stood condemned to death for their sins. The Lord of glory became incarnate and paid the death penalty for our sins. Once any law has exacted the death penalty it cannot do so again. In fact it becomes inoperative in relation to the one it has executed. If we are joined to Christ by faith in His finished work, we share in His fulfillment of the righteous demands of the law. The law has killed Him and us and we are therefore no longer subject to the law. Just as a woman whose husband dies is no longer bound to him but is free to marry another, so we being freed from the law by the interposition of death are freed to be joined to another. With this orientation, "I through the law am dead to the law" takes on profound significance.

Verse 20 is one of the most magnificent verses in all of
Scripture. It makes abundantly clear the fact that Christianity is not a matter of some legalistic form—of carefully
checking off a list of dos and don'ts. It is a life. Moreover, it is not human effort trying to bring off a superior
kind of morality but divine life surging through the individual. "Old things are passed away . . . all things are
become new" (2 Co 5:17). Verse 20 expands on the meaning of verse 19; Paul died to the law because he has been
crucified with Christ; he lives to God because Christ lives
in him. "I am crucified with Christ." The tense is perfect in
the Greek with the resultant meaning: "I have been and
remain crucified." This is how one dies to the law (v. 19).
Romans 6:1-6 linked with 1 Corinthians 12:13 explains
how one may be reckoned as crucified with Christ. By
means of the Holy Spirit we are baptized into one body
and into Christ. The Holy Spirit joins us to the church
(the body of true believers) and to Him and causes us
positionally to participate in His substitutionary death,
burial, and resurrection. The old man or old nature with
all its affections was crucified (Ro 6:6).

Because I have been raised to newness of life, *I live*.
But in a sense it is not *I* that live. It is not I in my own
strength that achieves in this business of living the Christian life. *Christ lives in me*. How stupendous! A member
of the divine Trinity living in me! Colossians 1:27 confirms the truth. But 1 Corinthians 6:19 adds the magnificent fact that the third Person of the Trinity also indwells
all believers. And superabundantly above, Colossians 2:9
observes that in Christ dwells all the fullness of the God-
head bodily. That means the whole Trinity dwells in Him

and us! (See also Jn 14:23; Eph 4:6; 2 Co 6:16.) What an antidote to discouragement, frustration, and weakness! ("We are more than conquerors through him that loved us" [Ro 8:37]). And what an antidote to returning to the "weak and beggarly elements" of the law (Gal 4:9). As I now live the Christian life, I shall not do successfully because Christ automatically operates in and through me. I live this life "in faith" (Gk) (the new sphere or rule of life—not in Mosaic law) which rests on "the Son of God." One must reckon in faith with or on the power which He supplies. In some mysterious, indefinable way the new nature or new I in the Christian must cooperate with divine power in living the Christian life. "Who gave himself." At the end of the verse comes a final reminder that the sacrifice of Christ is ultimately responsible for all that the Christian is and all the blessing he enjoys.

Now the apostle sets forth something of a summary of his position. "I do not frustrate" ("set at nought" or "make void" or "set aside") the grace of God as Peter or the Judaizers have been doing. He would not think of denying the validity of God's grace, which includes satisfaction of God's justice and the provision of justification on the basis of Christ's substitutionary work. If righteousness ("justification") came "by means of the law," then "Christ died needlessly" or without just cause. If there was the faintest possibility that man could procure his own righteousness, then the death of Christ was unnecessary. If the law could improve the standing of those who observed it as a rule of life, then Christ's death did not satisfy the law and introduce a new and better relationship. The fact that He died proves the need for His sacrificial death and the inability of man to achieve his own justification. Actually there are just two religions in the world: salvation by grace through faith in the finished work of Christ, and salvation by man's effort. Unfortunately too much passes for Christianity that smacks of the latter. And the problem of watering down the true faith came early. Paul's blistering attack upon it calls forth his finest efforts in this epistle.

4

JUSTIFICATION BY FAITH AS THE BASIS OF CHRISTIAN LIBERTY

3:1—4:31

Having defended his apostleship and the authority of his message, Paul now goes on to vindicate the truth of his message. In chapters 3 and 4 he asserts this truth by successive appeals to experience, to Scripture and to reason.

JUSTIFICATION EVIDENCED IN INITIAL EXPERIENCE OF THE GALATIANS (3:1-5)

In a word, Paul's message to the Galatians here is that their reason and experience should have convinced them of the all-sufficiency of faith. He breaks into a remonstrance at the beginning of this chapter. "O foolish Galatians" means not that the Galatians were naturally stupid or senseless but that they have been foolish in allowing themselves to come to the place of denying the sufficiency of Christ. Paul declares the mixture of law-keeping with faith in Christ irrational and implies that they should have been able to come to this conclusion themselves. "Who hath bewitched you" indicates that their conduct almost makes one believe they have been subject to some occult influence, popularly called "the evil eye." It would especially seem that they were under a spell when before their eyes "Jesus Christ hath been evidently set forth," that is, "placarded" or "proclaimed" as the crucified one. This "placard" should have been sufficient to ward off the evil eye. The sight of the crucified Christ ought to have counteracted all fascination with legalism.

As Paul begins his appeal to the Galatians, he is willing to rest his case on one issue alone, so telling is his argument. "This only would I [your teacher] learn of you. Received ye the Spirit by the works of the law, or by the hearing of faith?" Verse 2 must be connected with verse 5 where it becomes evident because of miracles occurring in their midst that they had received the Holy Spirit. On the face of it, reception of supernatural spiritual power on the basis of natural or human effort would appear impossible. In this case such reception would seem even more impossible because the Galatian church was essentially Gentile and hence had no special covenant claim on God (as did the Jews) nor a tradition of worship of God. Of course they knew very well that their salvation and accompanying spiritual power had come by *faith,* of which they had heard in preaching, that is, by Paul. The question the apostle raised was rhetorical and presumes the Galatians were not reflecting on what God had taught them as believers.

Verse 3 continues the questioning. "Are you so foolish?" Are you so irrational? You must acknowledge that your salvation and spiritual power came on the basis of faith. Having begun "in the sphere of the spirit" do you now wish to be perfected "in the sphere of the flesh," that is, to go into the keeping of ordinances? Of course their conversion experience had brought about a spiritual change. Now apparently some were arguing that a really spiritual person should keep the law. This was to exalt flesh above spirit, to ignore spiritual enablement for daily living, and to violate what Paul must have clearly taught them when present with them (cf. Phil 1:6; 2 Co 8:6).

If one accepts the South Galatian theory, he will find numerous indications of persecution among the Galatians at an early time. Trouble started in Antioch of Pisidia almost immediately (Ac 13:45, 50). The same was true in Iconium (Ac 14:2, 5) and Lystra (Ac 14:19). In each case Jews stirred up the persecution; it was too early for official persecution on the provincial or imperial level. No doubt persecution continued after the apostles left. Having suffered so much at the hands of the Jews, would the Galatians now turn to law-keeping, intimating that their former position in grace was erroneous and rendering all their former persecution *vain*, that is, "of no purpose"?

As Paul continues to appeal to the Galatians, he asks another rhetorical question: Does the miraculous work of the Holy Spirit depend on the works of the law or on the hearing of faith? He that ministers the Spirit is of course the Father. "Ministereth" is a very weak translation of a word better rendered "liberally supplies." God the Father liberally supplies the Spirit and by the Spirit works (Gk, energizes) in you supernatural powers (not to be restricted to visible miracles but applied more broadly to spiritual power). Does the Father bestow this blessing as a result of the works of the law or the hearing of faith?

The former would be impossible historically because the Galatians did not really know the law when they received the gifts of the Spirit. It is likewise impossible theologically because nowhere in Scripture is spiritual enablement bestowed on the basis of human effort. Of course a negative answer is expected to the first part of this rhetorical question.

JUSTIFICATION EXPERIENCED BY ABRAHAM (3:6-9)

In his attempt to prove the doctrine of justification by faith, Paul appealed first to the experience of the Galatians. Next he tried to show that his doctrine was exemplified in Abraham. Jews or Judaizers would have high regard for Abraham as being in some sense their progenitor. No doubt the Judaizers were urging the Galatians to be circumcised as Abraham had been. Paul appealed to them on the basis of the fact that the sons of Abraham were not under law but under promise. After all, Abraham lived before God gave the law to Moses. "Abraham believed God, and it was accounted to him for righteousness" is a direct reference to Genesis 15:6. The Genesis pronouncement follows immediately on God's promise of an heir in whom the Abrahamic covenant would be fulfilled (cf. Gen 12:1-3; 13:14-18). This, then, is what Abraham believed. It involves a dim view of something wonderful that God would do through him. Certainly one should not read too much into this passage. There is no evidence that Abraham saw Christ hanging on the cross for him, as one sometimes hears from the pulpit or a Sunday school class lectern. Abraham's faith is more wonderful because he had so little to go on. Essentially his faith was anchored in the person of God and His promises. Abraham committed himself totally and unreservedly to his God. "It [his believing] was accounted to him for righteousness." That which (righteousness) was reckoned over to his account was not his originally or naturally but was bestowed by God on the basis of faith. Works were not involved in obtaining justification. To be sure, Abraham offered his only son and did many other things at a later time that proved his faith; but he was not justified by those acts. He was justified by faith *before he performed* the good works. This lesson should not have been lost on the Galatian Judaizers.

Following logically from the discussion about Abraham's justification, the apostle says "you perceive" or "know therefore." There is some debate as to whether one should understand the verb to be imperative or indicative; the latter seems preferable. "They which are of faith" are those whose starting point or fundamental principle is faith. "The same," that is, these and these alone (in contradiction to "those of law") are "children [Gk, sons] of Abraham." If some were claiming to be sons of Abraham, then they must bear resemblance to their forefather. He was a man of faith, whose faith was declared to be the basis of acceptance before God. On one occasion Jesus appropriately reminded His hearers: "If ye were Abraham's children, ye would do the works of Abraham" (Jn 8:39). These words would be quite apropos for Paul's hearers at this moment.

Having established Abraham's justification by faith and the justification of his spiritual descendants on the same basis, Paul now returns to details of the Abrahamic cov-

enant, which anticipated Gentile salvation. The use of
scripture points to inspiration (cf. v. 22). "Scripture having foreseen . . . announced" is more than a personification
of Scripture. The sacred text is identified with the mind
that inspired it, with God Himself. God who inspired
Scripture foresaw that Abraham would be a source of
blessing to the Gentiles in New Testament times and after-
ward. He proclaimed the word orally to the patriarch and
inspired Moses to record that oral message some six hundred years after it was uttered. The writer of Scripture
foresaw that God would declare the Gentiles righteous as
a result or consequence of faith. Of course God justifies
Jews on the same basis, but Gentile salvation is in question
here.

So, having foreseen this marvelous truth, "God announced
as good news in advance to Abraham: 'In thee shall all
the Gentiles be blessed.'" Abraham was not given the
full revelation of what the gospel was but only the word
that all the Gentiles were to be blessed in him. "In thee"
indicates that from his line blessing would flow to "all the
Gentiles," a veiled reference to the Messiah. The Hebrew
of Genesis 12:3 has "all families of the earth." What the
blessing was can only be understood in connection with
the first part of the verse; it has to do with justification by
faith. Justification came to Abraham by faith in the promise; justification comes today by faith in the Fulfillment of
that promise. The apostle now concludes, "So then those
and those alone who are of faith [as the source of their
spiritual life] shall be blessed together with believing
Abraham" (v. 9). The conclusion here is the same as in
Acts 15: Gentiles are justified by faith and are heirs of

Abraham's promises apart from becoming circumcised and keeping the law. Gentiles are blessed *as Gentiles.*

DELIVERANCE FROM LAW-WORKS THROUGH CHRIST (3:10-14)

Paul now proceeds to show the impossibility of justification by the law, and deliverance from the works of the law through Christ. He had a reminder for Jews who held that their submission to the law entitled them to special blessings as sons of Abraham. "As many as are of [whose manner of life is characterized by] the works of the law are under a curse." Those who are under the law stand condemned rather than blessed or justified. The apostle quotes Scripture to prove his point: "Cursed is every one that continueth not in all things which are written in the book of the law to do them." This is a quotation of the Septuagint translation of Deuteronomy 27:26 with a slight change. Some argue that Paul means here to sum up in a single sentence the curses pronounced from Mount Ebal (Deu 27:15-26). It has been written and stands true to the present (Greek perfect tense) that a person under the law is cursed if he fails to render perfect obedience to the law ("in all things") continually or continuously ("continueth"). Hardly would a Jew claim to have kept the law perfectly; much less would Gentile pagans such as the Galatians, who were guilty of serious infractions of the law. Lawbreakers are subject to divine wrath and wait for the final destruction. Judaizers are under the curse; why should the Galatians share their fate?

If no one has kept the law fully, then all are condemned by the law. Thus it is evident that no one can be justified by law-keeping (3:11). "The just shall live by faith," the apostle avers, as he quotes Habakkuk 2:4 (cf. Heb 10:38). In doing so he shows that even under law (for Habakkuk wrote during the dispensation of law) the way of faith was superior to the legal way. The law could only condemn, not save. There has been considerable discussion on how to translate and to understand the quotation from Habakkuk. Perhaps a suitable rendition would be: "By faith shall the righteous live." Emphasis should be placed on faith because that is the apostolic focus of attention in this passage. Faith (in Christ and His work) is the basis of justification. *Faith, justification* (being declared righteous), and *live* are all simultaneous. As a believer exercises faith he is justified and receives life. Then he goes on to live the Christian life by faith.

Underscoring the point just made, Paul declares that the law has not faith but works as the fundamental principle of its existence (v. 12). Unfortunately, "The man that hath done them shall live in them." This rather free quotation from Leviticus 18:5 spells out the need for perfect performance under law to win divine approval. But if, as is true, this performance is more than we can accomplish, then we must cast ourselves on God in *faith*. In contrasting law and faith Lenski well observes:

> Faith has justification and life the instant it begins; doing law-works would get life only when the doing is ended and complete. But the point Paul makes is that faith and doing are opposites. Doing furnishes what is legally and of right *demanded*; faith receives what is gratuitously bestowed.[1]

Paul now gladly turns to the positive side of his argument: "Christ has redeemed us from the curse of the law." To redeem is to pay the purchase price. It is as if Christ entered the slave market and paid the required number of *sesterces* (Roman coin) for the one in bondage. In numerous passages the price is paid to ransom one from the slave market of sin. Here enslavement is viewed as being to the curse of the law. *Us* is frequently applied by the commentators primarily to the Jews, but it would seem to refer to Paul, those with him at the time of writing and those addressed—both Jews and Gentiles. The question may then be asked as to when Gentiles came under the Mosaic law. It may be answered that while the article is used before "law" in the Greek of verse 13, seeming to refer to the Mosaic law, the article does not appear before "law" in the Greek of verses 2, 5, 10, and 11. Hence commentators have observed that reference in this context is not limited to Mosaic law but refers to righteous law in the abstract. God makes righteous demands on all—Jew and Gentile alike. All who cannot meet the righteous demands of God (all men) are under the curse. This becomes quite clear in Romans 2:12-16 (cf. Gal 3:10: "As many as depend on law-works are under the curse").

Christ was "made a curse for us" in the sense that He was born under the law and became sin for us. The curse of death for sin came upon Him, and His substitutionary death on our behalf released us from the curse (see 2 Co 5:21; Is 53:6). The last part of verse 13 is quoted from the Septuagint of Deuteronomy 21:23. His bearing this particular curse is a sample of the general curse He bore. The Deuteronomy passage does not imply that Jews used

crucifixion as a method of execution; the Romans did that.
The Jews did, however, as a mark of ignominy hang bodies
on a post or stake (not a tree) by the hands after the individual had been killed in some other way.

Christ became a curse for at least two reasons detailed
here. (1) "That unto the Gentiles the blessing of Abraham might come in Jesus Christ." The promise had been
made in the Abrahamic covenant that in Abraham all families of the earth would be blessed (Gen 12:3). As noted
above, this fulfillment was possible only in and through
the person and work of the infinite Son of God, Abraham's
greater son. The blessing of Abraham or blessing promised
to Abraham involved, among the many national blessings,
the universal blessing of justification by faith. (2) "That
we might receive the promise of the Spirit through faith."
We again must refer to Paul, his associates, and the Galatians, and of course other believers. Paul has already (v.
2) made the Galatians admit that they had received the
Spirit by faith and not by works. Reception of the Spirit
is of crucial importance. Indwelling of the Spirit is a mark
of salvation (Ro 8:9; 1 Co 6:19). The Spirit bestows gifts
and enables us to live the Christian life. The coming of
the Spirit to indwell His people in some marvelous new
way was indispensable for the power and success of the
Christian church (cf. Lk 24:49; Jn 14:16-26; Ac 1:5, 8;
2:4). The promise of a great outpouring of the Holy Spirit
had been made long before Jesus' incarnation (Joel 2:28-
29), but that prophecy has at present been only partially
fulfilled. We wait until the end times for complete fulfillment.

INABILITY OF LAW TO ALTER THE COVENANT WITH ABRAHAM (3:15-18)

In his effort to show beyond a doubt the truth of justification by faith, Paul now argues that the Mosaic covenant, which came after the Abrahamic covenant, could not alter or destroy the unconditional covenant with Abraham. He observes (v. 15) that among men when a covenant is ratified no one sets it aside or amends it, neither the author nor a second party. Of course the implication is that if this is true with men it is even more true with God. A second covenant, the law, could not set aside the promise made to Abraham.

The Abrahamic covenant involved not merely a special blessing to Abraham that might ultimately be realized in such a way as to vindicate his name or enhance his reputation. The "promises" were made "to Abraham and his seed." The promises were not only spiritual, as noted above, but material—detailing specific blessings to a literal Israel in a specific land forever (Gen 12:1-3; 13:14-17; 15:1-6, 18). And the promises were made to "Abraham and his seed." The verse stresses the point that the promise focused primarily on one, namely Christ. Genesis 13:15 and 17:8 do specify *seed*, a collective noun. What the verse teaches is that the promises were not to all families descended from Abraham but to one special chosen family. Clearly Ishmael, Esau, and Midian did not participate in the blessing as did Isaac, Jacob, and Judah. There was a holy family or line of promise extending from Abraham down to Christ. Of course the Abrahamic covenant was to be abundantly fulfilled in Christ. Only under the personal rule of the infinite Son of God on Mount Zion will the descendants of Abraham occupy the promised land "forever." Only in the infinite Son of God could all the families of the earth be blessed. But Christ is viewed in this chapter as also being the head of a new family; all who receive Him by faith become sons of Abraham in a spiritual sense, as well as sons of God (cf. Gal 3:28-29).

The Abrahamic covenant, confirmed or ratified by God ("in Christ" does not appear in the best manuscripts), cannot be set aside by law, which came later (v. 17). The nature of the Abrahamic covenant must be properly understood. The Greek word is *diathēkē* which, strictly speaking, is not a contract between two parties but is more like a binding will or testament instituted by the first party. In this case God made unconditional promises to Abraham. While some may argue that the fulfillment of the Abrahamic covenant was conditioned on his obedience to God, that can hardly be admitted. But if it should be admitted for the moment, Abraham was after all obedient. Hence no further conditions hinder ultimate fulfillment of the covenant. The law, or Mosaic covenant, instituting the concept of blessing for obedience and cursing for disobedience, could not set aside the unconditional Abrahamic covenant.

The 430 years referred to here obviously applies to the period of time in Egypt (given in round numbers as 400 in Gen 15:13; Ac 7:6). That the law came 430 years after promise must mean that the law was given on Mount Sinai 430 years after the end of the age of promise. The latter ceased when the patriarchs left Palestine at the invitation of Joseph. The legal arrangement introduced could not set aside or alter the unconditional covenant made earlier. A most startling and amazing truth now comes clear. The age of law was merely a parenthesis between the age of promise and the age of grace, the latter being a continuation of the former. Believers today are children of Abraham by faith. The law was fulfilled and done away in Christ. All of the legalistic teaching the church has endured for nearly two thousand years is entirely incompatible with the teachings of grace and the spirit of promise. Perhaps the law cannot alter or set aside promise but legalists for centuries have been doing a good job of smothering the principles of Christian liberty which God Himself has ordained. The assertion that legalism is not the principle on which the Christian life operates must not be construed to mean that grace is lawless. A very instructive passage is Titus 2:11-12, which may be translated, "The grace of God . . . hath appeared to all men, disciplining us."

If the inheritance (i.e., spiritual privileges for Gentiles) springs from the law, it is no longer of promise because the two are fundamentally different in nature. *Law* and *promise* both appear without the article here and designate two opposing principles. "But to Abraham [Greek order] God gave [the inheritance] by promise." He not only promised the inheritance but gave it. *Gave* in the Greek perfect tense signifies "freely gave in the past and the bestowal remains in force at present."

TRUE PLACE AND PURPOSE OF THE LAW (3:19-29)

If the law is antithetical to promise and is not in force for the believer now that Christ has come, what good is it?

What function did it serve? Paul hastens to explain: "It was added because of transgressions." Rendall clearly explains the significance:

> The real meaning is that it was added with a view to the offences which it specifies, thereby pronouncing them to be from that time forward transgressions of the Law. Its design is gathered in short from its contents. The prohibitions of the Ten Commandments reveal their own purpose: they were enacted in order to repress the worship of false gods, idolatry, blasphemy, Sabbath breaking, disobedience to parents, murder, adultery, theft, false witness, covetousness. These sins prevailed before the Law, but by pronouncing them to be definite transgressions it called in the fear of God's wrath to reinforce the weakness of the moral sense and educate man's conscience.[2]

The law was added until the seed should come and was therefore a preparatory dispensation ending with the coming of Christ. While the promise was given to Abraham, "the friend of God," directly, the law was ordained or established by a mediator. In fact, a double mediator is mentioned: angels as representing God and Moses as representing the people. In his hand Moses received the tables of the law. No doubt Paul intends here to give an inferior place to the law by showing that it came through a mediator while God addressed Abraham directly. Moreover, the law was temporary, until the seed should come; and the function of the law was to convict of transgression, while the function of the promise was to remove the penalty of sin.

Verse 20 is very difficult to interpret; differences of viewpoint run literally into the hundreds. Each half of the verse has its own special problems. Two commentators appear to this writer to have approximated the true meaning. In regard to the first clause, "Now a mediator is not of one," Williams says: "i.e., does not belong to the category of 'one.' In a promise God acts alone; when a mediator is employed in any act of His there is an implication of plurality and separation from Himself so long as the thing mediated is in force."[3] Of course we must hasten to add that while Christ is referred to as a mediator in Scripture, He is not viewed as inferior to or different from God. He is very God; He is the man Christ Jesus (1 Ti 2:5).

As for the second half of verse 20, "but God is one," Rendall has a commendable interpretation which he likens to the message of Romans 3:30:

> The Apostle is there urging the real harmony of God's dealings with Jews and Gentiles, however different the method employed for justifying the two severally; and argues that it is nevertheless one and the same God who will justify both. So here after differentiating the revelation made through Moses from that to Abraham, he is careful to add that the God of Sinai is one with the God of Abraham, however distinct might be the two revelations. The true force of the clause may be expressed as follows, *but the God* (sc. the God of Sinai) *is one with the God of promise.* The twofold revelation of the name of God to Moses as the God of Abraham, Isaac and Jacob, and as the eternal God *I am that I am,* suggests the same thought of the divine unity in spite of the various aspects in which God reveals Himself to successive generations of men.[4]

If the law is inferior to promise, is there opposition between these two divine arrangements? Paul says, "Perish the thought." The law is all right as far as it goes, but it really could not compete with promise because it could not give life. The law as an externally prescribed rule cannot even pretend to impart life. And if sanction were given to law as a new means of justification, it would achieve nothing unless it gained a means of bestowing spiritual life.

"But," in contradiction to the idea that law might justify, its function is to "conclude all under sin." The picture here is variously painted by translators as "shut up like fish enclosed in a net," "enclosed entirely by barriers," and "shut up on every side as in a prison" (cf. Is 24:22). "All," not all men but "all the things," doubtless everything pertaining to men—their thoughts, words, and deeds—who are all sinners. They are all locked up and thus doomed under sin. The specific scripture referred to here is probably Deuteronomy 27:26 (cf. Ro 3:9, 19; 11:32) because it puts a curse on all who fall short of perfect obedience. "That." The law thus paves the way for fulfillment of the promise to all who put their faith in Christ. A paraphrase of the last part of verse 22 might read like this: "That the promised inheritance which is by faith in Jesus Christ might be freely given to those who believe in Him."

In verses 22-24 the preparatory feature of the law is emphasized. In verse 22 the law shuts up all under sin and paves the way for fulfillment of the promise. Here the law constrains or pushes men along unto faith. In verse 24 the law as a pedagogue leads men to faith. "Before faith came" is an inadequate translation; faith had been present on earth since Adam. The definite article appears in the Greek and the translation should therefore read "the faith." Reference is of course to faith in the person and work of the incarnate Christ alluded to in the previous verse. "We were kept under law." *We* could include all Jews or especially all believing Jews who were kept in ward or subjugated to control of the law. The verb often has the connotation of protecting rather than incarceration for punishment. Probably the word should be so understood here. God protected His children from the excesses of the heathen by controls of the law. "Shut up unto the faith afterwards to be revealed" indicates that the aim of this protective function of the law was to constrain or urge or push men to faith. The law was certainly no refuge; there could be no real refuge in anything but faith.

The King James translation of verse 24 does not give a clear idea of the intended meaning. In the Greek the law is called *paidagōgos*, not a *didaskalos*. In other words, the law was an inferior slave or servant (*paidagōgos*) committed with the task of bringing the master's son to school or to the schoolmaster (*didaskalos*). The pedagogue was charged with disciplining the child and giving him a moral training, with protecting him and regulating his outward habits. That was all the law could do; but when it led the son to Christ, its work was finished. In reality Christ was the schoolmaster (*didaskalos*); the translation has confused the picture or illustration, which would have been clear to a Roman of the day.

"Now that the faith has come, we are no longer under a pedagogue" (v. 25). Christ has come in the line of Abraham (see the genealogies in Mt 1 and Lk 3), fulfilling the promise to the "father of the faithful" and providing sal-

vation by faith in His finished work. The law has done its
work in showing the sinfulness of sin, in acting as a social
control in Israel, in bringing men under condemnation and
driving them to Christ. And Christ has fulfilled the law.
Therefore we are no longer under this pedagogue; its
office has ceased. The law in its preparatory ministry has
not been against or contrary to promise (v. 21) and now
will not be unless men insist on putting themselves under
law after grace has come.

In verse 26 there is a sudden shift in person from the
first to the second person plural. Emphasis in previous
verses has been primarily on the relation of Jews to the
law. With the coming of Christ, Abraham's seed in whom
all families of the earth will be blessed, Gentiles have
ready access to the spiritual blessings of God. Paul turns
to his largely Gentile converts in Galatia with the assur-
ance: "For ye are all the sons of God by faith in Christ
Jesus." Under the dispensation of law a child is represented as in the care of the pedagogue who will lead him
to the schoolmaster. Now that Christ has come, the believer in Him is an adult son (not *child* as in the English
translation), no longer under some kind of inferior tutelage. Perhaps "by faith" should be underscored because
again and again the apostle means to emphasize faith as
opposed to works in this epistle. And it might be added
that those who are viewed as sons are sons only by faith.
Those who have not put their faith in Christ are not sons
of God. There is no room in Scripture for a universal
fatherhood of God and universal brotherhood of man.

The exalted position of the son of God by faith now becomes clearer. Those who have received Jesus Christ by

faith "have been baptized into Christ." They have been linked to Christ in a living union and made positionally to participate in His death, burial, and resurrection (Ro 6:3-4). In the process they have also "put on Christ" or "clothed yourselves in Christ." Here is a reference to a highly significant ceremony that meant much to every young Roman man. When he came of age he was invested with the *toga virilis,* which signified that he was now a grownup son enjoying full citizenship with the rights and responsibilities pertaining thereto. He was no longer treated like a child in his father's household. The figure helps to explain how one becomes an adult son in the divine family (v. 26). He is joined to Christ by the Holy Spirit and clothed upon with Christ's robe of righteousness, by which means he can stand before God without fear of condemnation. To give the figure a slightly different orientation, when the Spirit comes to dwell in the individual he becomes a son of God. He is not brought into bondage again but is adopted by the Spirit into the family of God (Ro 8:14-16).

Now this family comes in for special attention. In it all are one in Christ; none enjoy superior Christian privileges. The Jew once was in a privileged position as a chosen, covenanted person; the Greek was simply one of the heathen. In the body of Christ spiritual or cultural antecedents do not impart particular advantages. A master may lord it over a slave, but in Christ social position does not grant special prerogatives. A beautiful example of the new relationship is seen in the case of the slave Onesimus who in Christ became a "brother beloved" to his master Philemon (Phile 16). Even sexual difference does not convey superior Christian privilege. To be sure, sonship in the new family does not erase religious, cultural, ethnic, social, economic, or sexual differences. But it provides a new bond of union, a new basis of fellowship, and a new equality of spiritual privilege. Regardless of his antecedents, one Christian finds Christ to be fully as sufficient as another.

"If you are Christ's." *If* might just as well be rendered "since," because there is no doubt of their salvation when they are sons of God, baptized into Christ, when they have clothed themselves in Christ and have been united in Him. Paul means to say something like this: "Since you [Gentiles, Galatians] are Christ's [not simply as servants but as members of His body], then you are Abraham's seed," for Christ is Abraham's seed. And this is so "according to promise," not according to the law. The apostle ends his thought where he began it in verse 7.

CONTRASTED POSITION UNDER LAW AND FAITH (4:1-7)

In these verses mankind is presented as a child, in a sense immature, until Christ's coming, when the guardian (law) was done away. As was commonly true in the testamentary systems of the Greeks and Romans, an heir as long as he was a *child* (here a minor at any stage of his minority) was no better off than a *slave* (and often was under the care of a slave), though he be *lord* of the whole estate by title and birthright. But he was under *tutors* (better, guardians of his person) and *governors* (better, stewards in control of property and household management) until whatever time appointed by the father. This age of maturity varied in different parts of the Empire and at different times. The exact age is of no importance to the present discussion; so we need not investigate the question here.

In verse 3 we come to the application the apostle seeks to make from this socio-legal arrangement. *We* refers primarily to Jews but must include Gentiles (Galatians) as well (cf. v. 5). The former were subject to the Mosaic law and the latter to the universal law of holiness (cf. Ro 2:12-16). We were spiritually *children* (minors), not the adult sons referred to in the latter part of chapter 3. Thus a remarkable change was wrought by the gospel—from a position of spiritual minors to adult sons. As just noted, not only Jews but also Gentiles in the spiritual immaturity of heathenism lived as children until the coming of Christ. Whether Jew or Gentile, all were under *bondage* until Christ came as the emancipator. "Elements of the world" were checks on the freedom of the heir as exercised by the guardians and stewards until he came of age (v. 2). Rendall well described the character of the elements.

> The association of this word with *nēpioi* [children] fixes on it the conception of a rudimentary training to which the world was subjected during its spiritual infancy by way of preparation for the Gospel of Christ and the dispensation of the Spirit. Before men could enter into the spirit of His teaching, they had to learn the elementary principles of religion and morality. Compulsory obedience to definite rules of justice and order was a necessary preparation for the freedom of the Spirit. This preliminary education was given to the Hebrews in the Ten Commandments and the Law, it was imparted to a wider world in Greek civilisation and philosophy, in Roman

law and government, and in other forms of national and social life. These rudiments are disparaged in ver. 9 as *weak and beggarly* in comparison with the teaching of the Spirit, for Christian men ought to have outgrown their spiritual childhood. So, again, in Col. ii. 8, 20, they are condemned wherever their traditional hold on human society produces an antagonism to the higher teaching of Christ. But before the Advent they formed a valuable discipline for the education of the world.[5]

"But when" marks the beginning of a tremendous change in the state of affairs. "The fulness of the time" occurred when world conditions were most auspicious for the coming of Christ and at a time appointed by the Father. Perhaps at no other point in world history could Christ and the church so effectively have swept onto the human stage. Culturally the Greeks had prepared the way for the coming of Christ and the church by providing a culture and a language which were adopted by Rome and spread throughout the Mediterranean world. Greek was the lingua franca of the Empire and could be understood by those who had access to New Testament literature and preachers of the gospel.

Politically Rome had prepared the way by uniting the Mediterranean world under one government and one citizenship. Ease of movement in that part of the world, facilitated by the marvelous Roman road system, is readily appreciated by the contemporary traveler who has no end of trouble with passports and visas; in fact, some countries in the Mediterranean area are periodically closed to him.

Religiously the Jews had made preparation by their preaching of monotheism in some one hundred fifty synagogues located throughout the Empire and by their anticipation of a Messiah who could solve the world's problems. Within Judaism, too, a preparation for the coming of Christ occurred as the law did its work and it became increasingly evident that no one could keep the commandments; the law "concluded all under sin." The philosophers made a religious contribution too, in a negative sort of way. They cast doubts on the old pagan systems of religion and looked for some sort of unifying power behind all of the old polytheistic systems of the day. At the most opportune time "God sent forth his Son." God took the initiative according to a divine plan. He sent His Son on the divine mission of providing salvation. The fact that He sent forth His Son demonstrates preexistence of the Son. Taking on human form so He could identify with fallen humanity, the Son was born of a woman. Born "under the law," He perfectly kept that law, fulfilled it, and ultimately paid its curse for all mankind.

"That he might redeem those under law" (Gk) is the reason why God sent His son. The Greek word for "redeem" is an especially beautiful term. The concept is of one going into the slave market and purchasing the slave and then taking him out of the market, setting him free. Of course if He redeemed those under the law and freed them, there was no reason why Gentiles who had never been under the law should now be under it. The law was no longer operative as a way of life for either Jew or Gentile. The result of redemption is *adoption* to divine sonship. The redeemed one is now an adult son of God, a man come of age, and is no longer a minor under guardians and stewards (i.e., *elements* or *law*).

It is one thing for God to assert that a person who has placed his faith in Christ enjoys an adoption to sonship in the family of God; it is another thing to give some evidence of the fact. The voice of the Holy Spirit within the believer confirms his sonship, and cries out to the Father in filial love. *Abba* is the Aramaic for father; whenever it occurs in the New Testament, it has the Greek interpretation added. When the believer has this subjective experience, he knows he is a son and no longer under the tutelage of a minor subject to legalism.

The Greek of verse 7 is much more expressive than the English: "So that (as a result of Christ's redemptive work on your behalf and His implanting the Spirit in your hearts) you are no longer (though you once were) a slave (in bondage under the law) but an adult son; and if an adult son (rather than one who is still a minor under certain controls), then an heir (enjoying a marvelous new spiritual heritage) through God [the preferred Greek textual reading]." "Through God" is very instructive. The entire Trinity has been involved in making the believer a son and an heir: the Father sent the Son who gave Himself to redeem us, and the Father implanted the Spirit in our hearts to act as a seal and an earnest (Eph 1:13-14) of our inheritance and aid us to live like sons of the King.

APPEAL TO GALATIANS TO TURN FROM LEGALISM
(4:8-31)

Appeal to avoid return to bondage, 4:8-11

Now that the apostle has shown the Galatians their exalted position as sons and heirs of God and therefore

free to enjoy spiritual adulthood, he next appeals to them
not to return to bondage. "Then," in their heathen state,
before their conversion, they "did service unto [Gk, 'were
enslaved to' or 'were in bondage to'] them which by nature are no gods." Men deified forces and phenomena
which by nature are not gods because they are not personal, rational, self-initiating, and omnipotent. Images
representing these forces and phenomena are not gods
either, for they possess no life or power. The reason why
the heathen were enslaved to that which was not divine
was that they "knew not God." This verse seems to conflict with Romans 1:21: "Because that when they knew
God, they glorified him not as God, neither were thankful;
but became vain in their imaginations, and their foolish
heart was darkened." The solution to the problem lies in
the employment of different Greek words for *know* in the
two passages. In Galatians 4:8 they knew not God as a
matter of inborn or innate knowledge. In Romans 1:21 the
text should be translated, "Because that when they came
to know God as a matter of experience, they glorified him
not as God." According to Romans 1:20 the Gentiles were
without excuse because they had had opportunity to observe the power and glory of God in His creation; but
having come to know Him or about Him in this way, they
chose to turn their backs on Him.

The Galatians did not know God by nature but they
came to know Him by personal experience (v. 9). They
came to enjoy a new relationship to Him as sons in a new
divine family. But just so they didn't try to take any credit
for the change, Paul reminded them that *rather* they had
come to be known by God. He had chosen them and pre-

destinated them unto the adoption of sons (Eph 1:4-5)
and attracted them by His Spirit to come to know Him
personally. In the light of this, how could they have
turned again to bondage? It is a real cause for wonder,
because they turned to the *weak* elements which had no
power to justify or enable one to live the Christian life.
They turned to the *beggarly* elements which were without
an inheritance or powerless to enrich. The *elements* or
rudiments of religion were just the ABC's; they had been
enjoying advanced studies. Did they want to be in bondage again to these weak and beggarly elements? As Gentiles they had suffered under the bondage of heathenism,
powerless to justify themselves and to please God. Now as
converted Gentiles, what did they want with a bondage
of Jewish legalism which was just as incapable of providing justification and spiritual enablement?

They meticulously observed special days with the belief that such a practice would gain merit, but this is entirely out of keeping with the spirit of Christian liberty.
Every day is to be lived for the glory of God. *Days*
(weekly Sabbaths), *months* (new moons or the especially
sacred first and seventh months), *times* (seasons, three
annual feasts of the Jews—Passover, Pentecost, and Taber-
nacles), and *years* (sabbatical or jubilee years) were not
enjoined on Gentiles. Of course Sunday is not a Christian
Sabbath; it is the first day of the week and worship on that
day celebrates the resurrection of our Lord. While the first
day of the week, like the seventh, has special significance
as a day for spiritual and physical refreshment, the first
day is not loaded down with prohibitions. But certainly
the believer should honor God on His day in corporate

worship. And he should avoid a "business as usual" approach to the day because he may by that means give the impression God holds no special place in his life.

"I am afraid of you" (v. 11), not because of personal fear but because Paul was apprehensive concerning the effect of their action on his work. If they continued in this legalistic pattern of life, all his efforts on their behalf would have gone for nothing, would be without any continuing and meaningful result.

Appeal from Paul's relations with them, 4:12-20

"Become as I, for I became as you, I earnestly beg of you." As a Jew, Paul was very faithful in keeping the law, but after his conversion he became like the Gentiles—no longer living under law. But a curious thing happened. The Galatians, who were not under law as Gentiles, after their conversion put themselves under the law as a way of life. So Paul pleads: I beg of you, come back out from under the law and live as I; enjoy your Christian liberty. When I ministered among you, at which time I lived as a Gentile rather than a Jew, you did me no wrong (did not *injure me*), you did not oppose me for that reason.

The first time Paul came among the Galatians he did not plan to stay for any length of time, but he contracted a serious illness and had no choice but to stay for a while (v. 13). During the period of recuperation he preached the gospel and many believed. This illness was probably malaria, which forced Paul from the lowlands around Perga to the highlands of Pisidian Antioch and other interior towns. There he could gradually recover and carry on some ministry. In spite of his weakness the Galatians

received him well. This siege of illness probably had
nothing to do with his "thorn in the flesh."

The Galatians did not succumb to the temptation to
despise either Paul or his message because of his illness
and his generally weakened condition (v. 14). Lenski
well observes, "A sick man is never impressive and assur-
ing. A sick man who claims miraculous powers and heals
others, while he himself remains sick, would certainly raise
serious doubts regarding any message he might bring."[6]
The Galatians did not reject Paul but received him as an
angel (as a powerful and glorious heaven-sent messenger
not plagued by illness), as representative of Christ Jesus.
Some have sought to find in this reference an allusion to
the scene in Lystra when Paul was taken for Hermes, the
messenger of the gods (Ac 14:12), but there seems to be
little to commend this identification of the two events. If,
however, it is correct to say that Paul did contract malaria
or some other fever in the lowlands and that he went
quickly to Antioch, then the events of Acts 13:42-44 must
have occurred when Paul was very low physically. On
that occasion, when the Jews failed to respond to the
gospel message, the Gentiles warmly urged Paul and Barnabas to preach to them: "And when the Gentiles heard
. . . they were glad, and glorified the word of the Lord:
and . . . many . . . believed" (Ac 13:48).

"What has become of your congratulation of yourselves?" (v. 15) is a better translation. They patted themselves on the back at having received Paul as an angel or
as Jesus Christ; what has happened to that feeling now?
The apostle freely bears witness to the Galatians of their
love. If possible they would have dug out their eyes and

have given them to him. So highly did they esteem Paul
that they would have made this tremendous sacrifice of
one of the dearest members of the body. Probably no reference is intended here to Paul's need of another pair of
eyes. Nor is there any real evidence that a partial loss of
eyesight was his thorn in the flesh (see comment on Gal
6:11). Those who assert that Paul was at this time suffering from a loathsome disfigurement of the eyes cannot
support their case. Disfigured individuals could not under
the prohibitions of Mosaic law fill positions of leadership
in Judaism. Yet Paul received an invitation from the elders
of the synagogue at Antioch to address them (Ac 13:15-
16).

"So then, have I become your enemy by telling you the
truth?" the apostle inquires. "So then" (Gk, hōste) is often
used to introduce a conclusion: in view of your change of
feelings toward me. "Have I become hostile" is a better
translation; the meaning is not "held in enmity by you."
In essence Paul asks, "Do you think I have become hostile
to you just because I have told you the truth?" Obviously
the Gentiles were well disposed toward him on his first
visit to minister to them; so apparently on the second journey he was forced to speak plainly to them about the Judaizing error and a barrier arose between them. It is not
our enemy but our best friend who makes the effort to tell
us the truth about ourselves.

Perhaps the Galatians had decided that Paul seemed to
be an enemy because he spoke the truth so plainly, but
now he warns them against flatterers who lead them astray
(v. 17). "They (the flattering Judaizers) zealously (with
great proselyting zeal) affect you (court you), but not

well." The Judaizers were neither worthy in themselves,
nor did they intend to further the true interest of the
Galatian converts. "Yea, they would exclude (shut out or
lock up) you, that ye might affect (zealously court) them."
They want to lock up or keep away or separate the Galatians from Paul and his associates and their influence and
teaching and substitute themselves for Paul in the affections of the Galatians so the Galatians would zealously
court them instead of Paul. Of course, in shutting up the
Galatians to themselves and their teachings, the Judaizers
were cutting the Galatians off from the true gospel and the
true church and breaking the blessedness of fellowship the
brethren had previously enjoyed.

Lest the Galatians conclude that Paul wants to monop-
olize their affections and their religious affairs, he says,
"But it is good to be zealously courted at all times in a
good thing and not only in my presence with you" (v. 18).
It is good for anyone to be eagerly sought after. It is good
for him psychologically to feel wanted. It is good for him
spiritually to be involved in God's work. There is nothing
wrong with being sought after; the issue is the purpose of
the seeking—for a bad cause (v. 17) or a good cause (v.
18). Moreover, one should be sought after in a good cause
"at all times," not sometimes for good and at other times
for ill. While Paul was with them they had sought after
him. Now that he is absent they are seeking after and
being sought after by others. But he will not be hurt if the
Galatians take up with others, as long as their course of
action is an honorable one. As in Philippians 1:15-18, his
only concern is that the gospel be preached and that God
be glorified.

While it may be good for the Galatians to be zealously sought after in a good thing, the truth is that they had not been. The Judaizers had turned them away from the gospel of grace. Now instead of addressing them as adult sons and heirs of God through Christ, Paul calls them "little children" and speaks of their need of a second spiritual birth. When he was with them the first time he had suffered birth pangs, as it were, until they were born unto newness of spiritual life from the bondage of heathenism. Now he is suffering birth pangs a second time ("again") until they are born unto newness of spiritual life from the bondage of Jewish legalism. "Until Christ be formed in you," until you become the sort of believers in whom Christ alone lives, must be linked with Galatians 2:20. The idea is that Christ shall take up His residence in the believer and so dominate every phase of his life as to mold that life. Such an experience would, of course, contrast dramatically with that of a believer whose religion consisted in externals governed by the law.

Paul's tenderness and concern for the Galatians, which extended to suffering birth pangs for their spiritual renewal, now expresses itself in his desire to be present with them if it were possible. It is hard to know exactly how their situation is when he must go on hearsay, and it is usually much more difficult to deal with a problem in writing than in person. If he were present he could change his tone of voice, either to suit the needs of the situation or to change from condemnation to praise. "For I stand in doubt of you" indicates distress of mind or perplexity or something similar in knowing how to deal with the

Galatians, whether firmly or gently, to bring them back to the standards of faith and grace.

Appeal from contrasted relationships, 4:21-31

From personal appeal Paul now turns to an illustration from Scripture in an effort to separate the Galatians from legalism. Those who boast of their submission to the law and claim to be sons of Abraham forget that Abraham had two sons, the one of a freewoman and the other of a bondwoman. Blessing and inheritance belong to the former. Paul declares the legalistic Galatians to be descended from the latter.

"You who want to be under law [probably the Mosaic law, though here without the article in Greek], do you not hear (or understand) the inner sense of the law [referring here in a broader sense to the Torah or Pentateuch]?" The inner sense of the Pentateuch concerns the history of an elect people descended from Abraham in the line of promise. Another son of Abraham, born of a bondwoman, prefigures legal bondage and was cast out. All the law can do is bring upon you a curse for sin and separate you from God. "Do you not hear" probably means in this instance (as in such passages as Mt 13:13) to hear and heed or obey, for Paul wants them not merely to listen to this illustration with historic or casual interest, but to learn a very special lesson from it.

"It is written [not a quotation but a summary of recorded facts from Gen 16:3-16; 21:2 ff.] that Abraham (whose sons ye wish to be) had two sons [he had others by a second wife—Gen 25:1-2—but those do not relate either to the line of promise or bondage], the one by a

bondmaid (Hagar, to whom was born Ishmael), the other
by a freewoman (Sarah, to whom was born Isaac)." The
status of the mother in each case determined the status
of the son.

The son born of the bondwoman was born "after the
flesh"—in the course of nature. Circumstances surrounding
Ishmael's birth were not ordained of God and were therefore natural. God would bring to fruition His own plan
in His own time without the aid of men or their con-
niving wives (Gen 16:1-2) who try to help His plans
along. Isaac was born of the freewoman "by virtue of the
promise" (Gk). He could not be born as a result of any
confidence in the flesh, because Abraham and Sarah were
both beyond the age of childbearing. Hence the promise
was miraculously fulfilled and salvation demonstrated to
be a work of God from start to finish (Jon 2:9), even to
the extent of providing a line in which the Redeemer was
to be born.

Paul does not deny the literal meaning of the Abrahamic narrative, but he says that the circumstances of the
history have another besides the literal meaning. Whether
"illustration," "parable," or "allegory" should be used to
describe the apostle's interpretation may be debated. Certainly Paul's use of this Old Testament account does not
give the contemporary Bible student license to allegorize
a variety of Scripture passages. It should be kept in mind
that what Paul says here is by the same inspiration as the
original Genesis account. Moreover, Lenski helpfully observes:

> Paul does not go a step beyond the Scripture facts; what
> he does is to point out *the same nature* in both: mere flesh

in Hagar's birth, and thus slavery—the same slavery in all
those whose birth is no better; divine promise in Sarah's
birth, and thus liberty—the same liberty in all whose birth
is connected with promise. Thus in v. 24-28 Paul identifies: Hagar = Sinai = the mother of all who do law-
works; Sarah = Jerusalem from above = the mother of
all believing the promise.[7]

"These (women) are (represent) two covenants (omit
'the')." The two covenants are of course the Abrahamic
and Mosaic. The one takes its origin from Mount Sinai
and brings forth children unto bondage. Paul identifies
the first and links it with the slave Hagar. Certainly the
last half of verse 24 would make a Judaizer squirm. The
reader is left to add a coordinate statement about the
Abrahamic covenant at this point. The apostle wants to
drive home the inferiority of Mosaic legalism.

The Greek text of the first part of verse 25 is difficult,
but probably we are to read: "For the Sinai mountain is
in Arabia." In any case, the idea is clear. Hagar fled into
Arabia twice (Gen 16 and 21), and her son and his descendants populated the Arabian region, of which the
Sinai peninsula is a part. The area has non-Jewish associations and has no part in the inheritance of the line of
promise. Sinai "answers to" or literally "belongs in the
same row or line with the present Jerusalem." It corre-
sponds in character to the earthly and visible Jerusalem
which is in bondage with her children. Both politically to
the Romans and religiously to the law, Judaism as centered in this city is in bondage. This Jerusalem, though
located in the promised land, still clings to law-works as if

she like Sinai were located in Arabia, outside the land of promise. Instead of an expected parallel to the last half of verse 24, introducing the other covenant, verse 26 launches into a statement about the Jerusalem above. A reasonably accurate translation of the verse would read: "But the Jerusalem above is free, in which character is mother of us." For centuries Jerusalem had been glorified in Hebrew history and hymnody as the capital of the Jewish commonwealth and a place where God especially chose to dwell. But the city had had her share of sin, sorrow, and bondage and had never come to enjoy the exalted place anticipated for her. Old Testament prophets looked forward to a golden age when the city would be free, when Messiah would rule in righteousness and holiness from Zion. When Paul wrote Galatians those prophecies had not yet been fulfilled. The city was still in political and spiritual bondage. In fact, it appeared that the old city would never realize the expectations so many had had for her.

Now Paul speaks of a "Jerusalem above" which is "free"; in the allegory or illustration Sarah, the free woman, answers to this Jerusalem. This "heavenly Jerusalem" is described in Hebrews 12:22-24 in terms of those present—the angels, redeemed persons, and Jesus Christ. The apostle John in Revelation looks forward to a time when the heavenly Jerusalem will come on earth, and he describes all the beauties of this city (Rev 21—22). Meanwhile, this heavenly city exists in its spiritual or invisible form as a brotherhood of believers free from the restraints of law because the love of Christ and the indwelling Holy Spirit constrain them to do the will of God from the heart. The heavenly Jerusalem which is free, as symbolized by Sarah, is "mother of us" (mother of all Christians already members of the invisible church). *All* is not in the best Greek texts. If it were, it would seem to imply that all regardless of nationality were identified with the Jerusalem above; this would introduce an extraneous concept here.

In verse 27 appears a quotation from the Septuagint (Greek translation) of Isaiah 54:1. The context of that verse is a triumphant anticipation of Israel's deliverance from foreign bondage and restoration to the land of Canaan. Attention is centered on a population greatly increased in restored Jerusalem beyond what it had been earlier. God's dealings with Abraham and Sarah became a kind of type of His dealings with their spiritual progeny. The intimation of the verse is clear: Sarah was to have spiritual descendants in far greater number than Hagar. That Paul does not merely pull a verse out of context and allegorize its meaning for his purposes, Williams makes clear.

> The prophet refers however to Zion in words transcending the fulfilment in the return from Babylon. Thus St. Paul's quotation is more than a play on words; it gives the essential part of the original meaning, that there is to be a Jerusalem other than that which we now see, and that the number of its children is to be far greater.[8]

"Rejoice thou barren" applies to Sarah who did not bear children "after the flesh," according to nature. After a long period of barrenness she bore a child according to promise; so she was to "cry" or shout for joy. The reason for exaltation was that "the desolate hath many more children than she which hath an husband." The desolate one, Sarah, who represents the promise, largely fulfilled in the New Testament church, will have many more children than would be subject to the covenant of law. The New Testament church is predominantly composed of Gentiles, once without the promise and without God as their husband. The Jews, on the other hand, had God as their husband. Though spiritual sons of Hagar, under bondage, were numerous, spiritual sons of Sarah, according to promise, would be far more numerous because encompassing Gentiles in the New Testament church.

"Now we, brethren, are, after the category of Isaac, children of promise" (v. 28). All the children of Sarah are members of one family. We, Paul and the Galatians, are brethren in this brotherhood of freedom. We are "after the category of Isaac"; if in the same category, we are children of promise. We are both its spiritual product and channels of the promise. The implication is that we are and ought to continue as children of promise, rather than trying to live as children of bondage.

If we are in the line of Isaac, we need not be surprised when persecuted by the seed of Hagar. "He that was born after the flesh (Ishmael) persecuted him born after the spirit (Isaac)." The one specific biblical indication of this animosity appears in Genesis 21:9. On the occasion of Isaac's being weaned, Abraham put on a banquet. Ishmael "mocked" Isaac, probably ridiculing his position as a child of promise and no doubt fearing lest the young lad preempt all the inheritance that the elder (Ishmael) felt was rightfully his. While physical harm does not seem to have been inflicted on this occasion, a tendency and disposition to persecution on the part of Ishmael became evident.

What was incipient in Ishmael became very real in his descendants. Those who would have an intelligent perspective on the current Arab-Israeli conflict should bear in mind that animosity between the two peoples has existed ever since the days of Abraham, and it will not be quickly dissipated in our time by surface solutions to deep-rooted problems.

"As then . . . so . . . now." Just as children of the bond-woman (Hagar) persecuted children of the freewoman (Sarah) in the past, so now children of bondage (Jews and Judaizers) persecute children of promise (e.g., Paul and the Galatians). With the exception of troubles suffered at Ephesus and Philippi, Paul and his associates endured all their persecution at the hands of Jews—in bondage to the law.

But as an encouragement to any believers who suffer opposition at the hands of those in bondage, Paul deduces a lesson from the Scripture. It very clearly states in Genesis 21:10, 12 that Abraham was commanded to expel Hagar and her son from the household and to cut them off from inheritance in the family. This comment was not only to be an encouragement to believers but a solemn reminder to Judaizers that mere observance of the law brings no abiding inheritance in the family of God. Lenski aptly observes:

> If the Galatians and we forsake the Gospel freedom for the slavery of the law and legalism we make ourselves one with Hagar and Ishmael, so that: "Throw them out—they shall not inherit!" becomes God's verdict on us. "God

forbid!" should be our answer to that. This is the real object of Paul's exposition.[9]

In verse 31 Paul draws his argument to a conclusion: "Wherefore, brethren, we are not children of a bondwoman, but of the free woman." *Wherefore* is a deduction from the preceding verses (21-30). The definite article does not appear before bondwoman but does before free woman, calling attention to the superiority of the latter. It is established then, that we (Paul and the Galatians) are not children of a bondwoman who was cast out from the presence of her lord and denied any share in the inheritance. But we are children of the free woman, children of the promise and according to Scripture heirs in the family of God.

5

CHRISTIAN LIBERTY IN PRACTICE
5:1—6:10

While Paul was certainly the most profound theologian who ever lived, he never divorced doctrine from life. Instead, he believed that doctrine should change life. In all of the apostle's letters to young churches, he first pens a doctrinal section and then follows it by a practical section. First he establishes his teachings and then discusses how to live in the light of those concepts.

THE CONSEQUENCES OF LEGALISM (5:1-12)

Verse 1 is a ringing exhortation to maintain Christian freedom. "For freedom Christ set us free" is a proper rendering of the first part of the verse, which links closely to 4:31 and the preceding illustration, or allegory. Freedom from bondage in Abraham, Sarah, and Isaac would be impossible without the work of Christ. Christ is the great liberator; He freed us from bondage unto a life of Christian liberty. While we cannot set ourselves free from bondage, there is a sense in which we must cooperate with divine power in living the Christian life. Although Christ lives in me (Gal 2:20), nevertheless I live; my will must

determine to keep standing firm in the hard-won liberty
which Christ has made available.

"Stop subjecting yourselves again to a yoke of slavery,"
the apostle further admonishes. Released from the bondage of heathenism, the Galatians were actually engaged in
the process of subjecting themselves "again"—to another
yoke, the Mosaic law. Harrison perceptively observes,
"In some ways it is easier to live as a slave than to make
right use of one's freedom (e.g., Israel in the wilderness
wishing to return to Egypt)."[1]

The apostle now turns to a major example of entangle-
ment in the bondage of the law: circumcision. Although
the Judaizers may have put little stock in his message, he
still claimed apostolic authority in making a fundamental
pronouncement. The statement "if you allow yourselves
to be circumcised" should not stand alone. It must be connected with purpose. Paul still practiced the rite for the
sake of conciliation (Ac 16:3); it could be looked upon as
a national rite. But it was quite another thing for Gentiles
like the Galatians with no background of circumcision to
submit to the rite. Harrison succinctly comments, "In their
case the rite could only signify a deliberate attempt to
create merit by adopting a legalistic position and seeking
righteousness by works."[2] So he who submits to circumcision for justification fears the law and disbelieves in the
all-sufficiency of grace. One cannot be saved by something
he disbelieves. To such individuals Paul declares: "Christ
shall profit you nothing"; that is, His provision of salvation
cannot really profit you if you do not fully trust in it.

But circumcision will not only deprive one of the bene-
fits of Christ's work on his behalf, it will also bring a new

obligation: to keep the whole law. "I testify" or witness
to the fact "again" is taken by some to refer to the previous
verse but more likely alludes to his ministry among the
Galatians after the Council of Jerusalem. On that occasion
he no doubt explained the council decision that the law
was not binding on Gentiles and included comments on
the implications of circumcision. Acts 15:1, 5, 24 clearly
indicate that the rite was at issue during the council. While
"every man" had special reference to those in Galatia, it
can apply to all men everywhere today. All who would
put themselves under part of the law as a system of righteousness are obligated to the whole law with its requirements and its curse. The fuller translation "who is in the
process of allowing himself to be circumcised" indicates
that the Galatian defection was not yet complete. Those
who try to keep the law are in real trouble, "For whosoever shall keep the whole law, and yet offend in one point,
he is guilty of all" (Ja 2:10; cf. Gal 3:10).

The first part of verse 4 almost defies translation. The
better attempts include: "your connection with Christ
became void" and "you are severed from Christ." The
main idea is "to make idle, inactive" so there are no results. Rendall comments that the word "denotes the paralysis of spiritual life by severance of union with Christ.
This paralysis produces a deadening effect on the whole
spiritual nature, and results in the continuous craving for
legal justification. . . ."[3] Actually the King James Version
does not provide a bad rendering: "Christ is become of no
effect unto you." The second part of the verse does not
teach that an individual can be justified by keeping the

law; the verb is better translated "would be justified" or "are seeking to be justified."

"Fallen from grace" has nothing to do with the Arminian doctrine that a Christian can lose his salvation. Whatever one may say about that subject in connection with other Scripture passages, it is not the topic of discussion here. If one has stood in grace he has fallen from it at the moment he seeks justification by legalism. To put it another way, if one is perched on the high platform of grace, he may be said to have fallen from it on to the ground of self-righteousness when he puts himself under law.

"For we." In grand contrast Paul introduces the experience of the true believer. Rather than groveling around on the level of works-righteousness with accompanying fears of acceptance before God, we by the Spirit "wait eagerly by faith for the hope of righteousness." Faith is a kind of catalyst that engenders a sure hope. While to "wait eagerly" usually has as its object the coming of the Lord (1 Co 1:7; Phil 3:20; et al.), here it envisions the realization of the hope of righteousness or justification. Of course that, too, will occur at His coming for those who are caught up to meet Him then; others will experience it when they go to meet Him. Although we are justified at once when we receive Christ as Saviour, there is a sense in which justification will be consummated when we see Him. The whole creation groans and labors under the curse of sin and the weakness of the flesh and looks forward to that wonderful day when man shall receive a new and glorious body and creation shall be redeemed from bondage. Paul elsewhere described it this way:

For the earnest expectation of the creation waiteth for
the manifestation of the sons of God. Because the creation itself also shall be delivered from the bondage of corruption into the glorious liberty of the children of God
(Ro 8:19, 21).

In that glorious day God will put the capstone on His pro-
gram of salvation. The full implications of divine justification will be revealed.

To the one "in Jesus Christ" (in union with Him by the
Spirit) neither circumcision nor uncircumcision is "valid"
or "capable of producing results" (v. 6). The question
raised here is not how one becomes a Christian but how
he lives as a Christian. In the community of believers,
neither seeking to follow the law nor seeking to live without it makes one a superior Christian. What is really capable of producing results in the life of the Christian is
"faith expressing itself in love." His faith brings him into
vital union with God who comes to live in the believer
and sheds abroad His love in the experience of the believer
and begets there a love to God and man. So, if as a believer he is impressed with the law and a legalistic approach, he must remember that the law is fulfilled in love
(Gal 5:14). And if he prides himself on being without
law, he must remember that this liberty does not free him
to walk after the flesh in a selfish manner; he must con-
sider others in love. In this sense neither circumcision nor
uncircumcision is capable of producing results. Love is
the operative principle governing Christian relations.

Verses 7-12 constitute an expostulation against false
teachers and their leader and against following erroneous
doctrine. "You were running well" introduces another of

Paul's metaphors taken from the athletic life of the Greco-Roman world. You began your race well; you started out well in the Christian life. "Who hindered you" means "to cut into," "to impede." The idea is, "Who has cut into your lane on the track" and caused you to stumble? Attention seems to focus on a leader of the false teachers rather than on Judaizers in general as is the case elsewhere. This individual had led them away from subjection to the truth of the gospel, which involved justification by faith and a life of Christian liberty. In this latter part of the verse Paul abandons the metaphor for the reality of his subject.

"This influence that has won you over came not from the one calling you" (v. 8). You obey not the truth but choose to obey the hinderers. Be assured that this persuasion has been due to merely human effort; it has not come from the one who called you at first unto salvation and continues to call you. Whatever voice you have been hearing, it is not the voice of God.

Verse 9 introduces a proverb quoted also in 1 Corinthians 5:6: "Alas, it takes only a little leaven to affect the whole lump," (Phillips) warns the apostle. Leaven became a type of moral and spiritual corruption because of its fermentation capabilities. In the 1 Corinthians reference leaven applies to the corrupting influence of a bad person; some would apply it here to the leader mentioned in verse 7, but it seems rather to speak of false doctrine. The proverb could refer here to the fact that observing the law in a few points would lead to observing it in more, or it could indicate that the Judaizing infection once admitted would spread. The latter is more probable. Apparently the heresy had not yet spread widely and Paul was with this epistle trying to eradicate the already existing leaven from their midst.

"I have confidence regarding you in the Lord" more accurately expresses the Greek than does the Authorized Version of verse 10. The apostle reminds the Galatians of his personal claims on their allegiance and asserts his confidence in their reception of his message because his confidence is really in the Lord, who is able to give power and persuasiveness to his arguments. "That you will not be otherwise minded" is susceptible of two applications: that they will not be otherwise minded than he bids them in this epistle or that they will not be otherwise minded than they were before the disorder broke out. Actually if the error is properly eradicated both would be true. "Whosoever (of whatever quality or class) troubles you shall bear his judgment." Every offender shall bear as a heavy burden his own judgment. Paul does not say "condemnation" but leaves the judgment indeterminant—with God who is the righteous judge.

"And I" (v. 11). Paul contrasts himself with the Judaizing leader scored in verses 7-10 and his experience with the accusations Judaizers hurled against him. For his part Paul did claim to preach a message that came from "him that calleth you" (v. 8). Apparently the Judaizing leader and others accused him of preaching circumcision and the law, in spite of his protests to the contrary. These taunts may have arisen because of Paul's circumcision of Timothy (Ac 16:1-3) and his presumed indifference to the practice of circumcision and other aspects of the law among Jews (Ac 16:4; 15:29; cf. 1 Co 7:18). He does not answer these

Judaizing taunts with any long theological discussion but simply puts a question to them. How is it I still endure persecution at the hands of law-keepers if I am preaching the law? There would be no reason to persecute Paul if he were preaching the same message as the Judaizers. If he did preach such a message the "offence of the cross" would cease as far as his ministry was concerned. As a matter of fact Paul did not preach circumcision as the ground of salvation but Christ crucified; therefore the offense remained. The offense, or stumbling block, of the cross exists in that it is against man's pride and ambition, for man does not like to think he needs salvation or that he cannot work for it. Paul's message always sought to give God all the glory for the solution to man's sin problem.

At the conclusion of this section on the consequences of legalism, Paul utters an outburst against those who were troubling the Galatian believers. *Trouble* is a very forceful word here. It speaks of turning them upside down, of upsetting the peace and order in the Galatian churches, and may even involve riotous or seditious conduct (Ac 17:6; 21:38). In the latter sense the Judaizing error is viewed as capable of overthrowing the whole divine system of salvation. The apostle expresses a desire that they be "cut off." Actually the Greek verb is in the middle voice, "cut themselves off." A few commentators apply this to the Judaizers' cutting themselves off from the Galatian communion as a worthless foreskin is thrown away. But the majority favor a stronger concept; as the RSV puts it, "would mutilate themselves." The Galatians would be familiar with this practice because votaries of Cybele frequently engaged in it. In his irony the apostle may be sug-

gesting that the Judaizers who are so interested in cutting
outdo themselves and castrate or mutilate themselves.
Harrison observes: "As an emasculated man has lost the
power of propagation, so should these agitators be reduced
to impotence in spreading their false doctrine. Such is the
fervent wish to which the Apostle Paul gives expression
here."[4]

THE LIFE OF CHRISTIAN LIBERTY (5:13—6:10)

The life of Christian liberty is directed by love, 5:13-15

As Paul now launches into his discussion of the life of
Christian liberty, he points out that liberty must not be
allowed to degenerate into license but should be governed
by love and consideration for others.

"For ye" reminds the Galatians that the Judaizers with
their upsetting dogmas of legalism were striking at the
very root of their faith. They had been "called" out by the
Holy Spirit from among a sinful and condemned humanity
"unto liberty." The latter is better translated "on the foot-
ing of" or "on the condition of" or "on the ground of freedom." In other words, freedom was an essential element
in the Christian life. But, he warns, do not make your
liberty an opportunity for giving way to carnal passions.
Do not make your liberty "a base of operations" for the
flesh in its war against the spirit. In such a case a man
may be brought into bondage to corruption. There are
three kinds of bondage described in this context: the bondage of legalism and bondage to the flesh or old nature,
both of which are condemned; and a bondage of love,
which is strongly urged. If one wants to be in bondage,

let him serve others in the bondage of love. Be bound by love in your service one to another. In other words, you are living on a plane of liberty or freedom, but you are not free to do exactly as you please. Some practices may be lawful but not wise; nor may they contribute to the welfare and spiritual development of others. The Galatians had been looking for a bondage. Now Paul recommends a real and worthwhile bondage for them to subject themselves to: a bondage of mutual love. Rendall puts it well: "The true ideal of the Christian is not freedom, but unfettered service to the love of God and man. . . ."[5]

"For." What follows in verse 14 justifies service to others in the bondage of love as just discussed. "For all the law is fulfilled [probably better, "finds its fullest statement" or "truest utterance"] in one word (in the observance of one precept): you shall love your neighbor as yourself" (cf. Lev 19:18). Of course love to God is presupposed because one cannot begin to love his neighbor as himself unless he first loves God and the love of God is flowing through him. Who constitutes one's neighbor is elaborated in part in the parable of the good Samaritan (Lk 10:29-37). While applying originally to Jews in Leviticus 19, *neighbor* in the view of Christ included anyone in need.

In verse 15 appears the opposite of what would be the case if all were done in Christian love. The exercise of Christian love would result in building up the body; the lack of it results in destruction. The verse at first glance almost seems out of place, but probably it provides a glimpse of the strife existing in some of the Galatian churches as a result of the Judaizing error. "If you bite (tear into another or backbite) and devour (exploit or

devour substance by extortion) one another, take heed
(be on your guard) lest you be consumed (lest your corporate testimony perish or your strength and resources be
consumed by broils)." The Christian ideal is a group of
believers indwelt by the Holy Spirit and dwelling together
in unity.

The life of Christian liberty is a walk by the Spirit, 5:16-26

The apostle's goal in this passage is to describe liberty
in daily life and how it is to be achieved. "Walk by the
Spirit" (v. 16) is the preferred translation. The difference
from the Authorized Version—"Walk in the Spirit"—is important. Walking *in* the Spirit implies more dependence
on self; walking *by* the Spirit properly emphasizes the
energizing power within. To walk by the Spirit is to allow
the Spirit to be the governing principle in one's life. If the
believer permits the Spirit to control, he shall not "fulfill
(give effect to or allow to be accomplished) the lusts of
the flesh (the natural man or old nature, distinct from
physical body)." Flesh is looked upon as evil in Scripture
but body is not. We shall never obtain new flesh but we
shall gain a new, incorruptible body at the resurrection.
The believer has no promise to be free from the lusts of
the old nature in this life, but he need not capitulate to
temptation (1 Co 10:13). The works of the flesh are enu-
merated in verses 19-21.

Verse 17 describes essentially the same struggle within
the believer as appears in Romans 6 and 7. Briefly the idea
is this. Within the believer are two natures, an old nature
and a new nature, a fleshly nature and a spiritual nature.
The first he receives at birth and the second by regenera-

tion. The term *flesh* encompasses all the desires of the natural man and *spirit* the desires of the spiritual man or regenerate or new nature. The old nature is still under the influence of the Prince of this world who energizes the children of disobedience (Eph 2:2). The new nature is enabled by the Holy Spirit to overcome the downward pull of the old nature. *Lusteth* is not a very meaningful translation today, for now it has an evil connotation; the term in the Greek is neutral. "Contends against" would not be a bad rendering, though it is not completely exact. The last part of the verse is commonly taken to mean that the old nature is so active that we find it almost impossible to accomplish the good things our new nature wants to achieve. But several of the commentators point out that the whole context is so gloriously positive and victorious that emphasis must be put on defeat of the flesh. Thus Harrison says: "Behind the Spirit's resistance to the flesh is the divine purpose that believers should be kept from doing things they (otherwise) would do."[6] And Lenski concludes:

> Paul says that *the result* of this clashing of flesh and spirit is that we do not go on doing (present, durative) what we may want to do. The indefinite relative clause means "What we may want to do" in carrying out some craving of our flesh. The spirit in us succeeds in blocking this. . . . It is this context which makes v. 17 differ from Rom. 7, 15 etc., where the victories of the flesh are recorded. These are not denied here, but here the victories of the spirit are the subject.[7]

At first glance verse 18 does not seem to follow directly

on the argument of verse 17, but let us take another look. "If you are led by the Spirit," if you are under the control of the Spirit, then of course the Spirit will be contending successfully against the flesh and its manifestations. You are therefore not under the condemnation of the law because the righteous demands of the law are being fulfilled in daily living by the ministry of the Spirit. Moreover, the Spirit is the seal of our being in Christ (Eph 1:13), and therefore we are no longer under condemnation of the law. We do not need an external curb to keep us in line or to produce righteousness, because the internal impetus (the Spirit) to righteousness is abundant. Furthermore, the law is made for the fleshly man, not for a righteous man (1 Ti 1:9).

Verses 16 through 18 spotlight the importance, yes, the necessity, of the Holy Spirit's ministry if the old nature or flesh is to be kept under control. Now verses 19-21 go on to detail the works of the flesh and show the heinousness of that nature and its potential for evil if left unchecked. Of course no one could hope for a life of liberty or freedom when faced by the enslaving power of such propensity to evil. The life of Christian liberty then must not only involve freedom from bondage to the law but freedom from enslavement to sin. This catalog of sins gives support to the concept of total depravity, but it should not obscure the fact that the old nature is capable of good works on occasion. The doctrine of total depravity does not teach that man is always as bad as he can be but that he is totally incapable of doing good works of the sort that will merit his justification.

The actual doings or works of the flesh are manifest or

open to public view and show the flesh to be what it really is. Lusts or fleshly cravings (v. 16) if allowed to go unchecked will lead to expression of this sort. "Which are these" might more accurately be translated "such as," "for example," or "of which kind." The point is, Paul does not view the sins here as any sort of complete listing but only as examples of the kind of evil the flesh is capable of. Paul on other occasions has focused attention on the evil tendencies of man; Romans 1:18-32 is a classic example (cf. 2 Co 12:20-21; Eph 5:3-4; Col 3:5, 8). Various classifications of these works of the flesh have been attempted. A fourfold division is followed here:

1. Sexual sins: fornication, uncleanness, lasciviousness (adultery does not appear in the best manuscripts)
2. Idolatry and magic
3. Sins of strife: hatred, variance, emulations, wrath, strife, seditions, heresies, envyings, murders
4. Sins of intemperance: drunkenness, revellings

The apostle sets at the head of the list sins involving continuation of the human race. *Fornication* involves all illicit sexual relations; *uncleanness* is a broader term including not only sexual irregularities but all that leads to them; *lasciviousness* denotes open shamelessness, insolent disregard of decency, or brazen boldness in this reprehensible kind of life. These three words appear together also in 2 Corinthians 12:21.

Idolatry, the open recognition of false gods, probably appears here because of the close connection between sexual immorality and heathen worship. Both male and female prostitution were often practiced if not enjoined by heathen religions. The tendency to idolatry arose not only from a superstitious predisposition but especially from the very nature of Greco-Roman society. Political rallies, public festivals, dramatic events, sports spectaculars, and other aspects of public life were associated with the worship of some deity (e.g., the Isthmian Games at Corinth were held in honor of Poseidon and involved sacrifice to him; at hospital or healing centers, Asclepius, god of healing, was worshiped).

Witchcraft (better, "sorcery"), is the translation of the Greek *pharmakia*, from which our word *pharmacy* comes. Condemnation here rests not on the use of medicine but on the fact that among pagans the use of drugs was regularly accompanied by occult practices. Drugs were commonly the media in the practice of magic or sorcery; so the word comes to signify secret tampering with the powers of evil.

Sins of strife are numerous. *Hatred,* the opposite of love, "enmities," has in view the mutual animosities of men. *Variance* is dissension or strife, not necessarily implying self-interest. *Emulations* is better translated "jealousy," which arises out of enmity. It has in view rivalry involving self-assertion. *Wraths* indicates an ascending scale of animosity; jealousy smolders until it erupts in wrath. Concerning these four terms, Lenski well observes:

> Four forms of *personal animosity* are listed. The first denotes personal hatreds or enmities; the second the strifes and wranglings that result; the third the motives so often involved, jealousies; the fourth the outbursts of hot passion in angers: the first and the third point to motives, the second and the fourth to their product.[8]

From personal animosity we move to factionalism. *Strife* (better, "factions"), results from the fact that when individuals clash, supporters line up behind them; the word involves the idea of bribery and winning over followers. Factions lead to *seditions* ("divisions"), and whole groups of people "stand apart" (lit. meaning) from each other. Unfortunately, these somewhat temporary divisions may become reasonably permanent and develop not only an external but also an internal separation as to aim and purpose and conviction (*heresies*). The Greek word *haireseis* soon came to apply not merely to a separate view or position but to false doctrine held by the separating group or sect. *Envyings* help to create false doctrines and the factions which they cause. *Murders* does not appear in the oldest manuscripts; but if the word is permitted to stand, it marks the climax of antagonisms.

The apostle singles out two sins of intemperance: *drunkenness* or drunken sprees (excessive indulgence in strong drink) and *revellings* (carousals, probably public revels such as those connected with the worship of Bacchus, the god of wine). Probably the former term has more to do with individual and the latter with corporate indulgence.

Paul had forewarned the Galatians and now he repeats his warning of the consequences of permitting such sins to be exercised freely in their midst. They who *do* (practice) things like this "shall not inherit the kingdom of God." Christians may and will sin occasionally; they will *do* wrong and upon confession shall be forgiven (1 Jn 1:9). But they who "practice" such things or continue to do them as a set course of conduct, that is, live in sin, shall not inherit the kingdom. The morally corrupt as a matter of fact "shall not" inherit the kingdom. This statement does not involve any question of earning salvation, which is always obtained as a free gift in Scripture; but if an individual lives in sin, that is good evidence he has never become a new creation in Christ and therefore shall not inherit the kingdom of God.

As verse 16 makes clear, if the believer walks by the Spirit he shall not fulfill the lust of the flesh. The tendencies of the flesh will not be permitted to mature into the full-fledged manifestation of the flesh just described. Instead, his life will be characterized by the fruit of the Spirit (vv. 22-23). John 15 has something to say about the believer being a branch in the vine, enjoying living union with Christ and enjoying divine life coursing through him to produce fruit. The believer does not himself produce the fruit; the divine power in him does. As the Christian walks by the Spirit, the outward manifestation of the fact will be "fruit of the Spirit." It is interesting to note here that fruit is in the singular, signifying the unity and peaceableness brought by the ministry of the Spirit. The works of the flesh are, on the other hand, plural, indicating their disorganizing and disorderly effects on the individual.

Just as there have been many attempts to catalog the works of the flesh, there have been like attempts to catalog the fruit of the Spirit. Lightfoot's outline is adopted here.[9]

1. Christian habits of mind in their more general aspect: love, joy, peace.

2. Special qualities affecting an individual's relationship with his neighbor: longsuffering, gentleness, goodness.

3. Principles which guide a Christian's conduct: faith, meekness, temperance.

Love is the foundation, is the mother of all other Christian graces. The Greek word here is not *eros* (sexual love) or *philia* (liking or affection) but *agapē* ("the love of intelligent comprehension united with corresponding blessed purpose"[10]). This kind of love involves self-sacrifice and self-denial without asking for something in return. Of course 1 Corinthians 13 is an especially beautiful exposition of this kind of love. The Phillips translation brings home the force of the original of the 1 Corinthians passage much better than the King James.

Joy (conferred by Christ Himself on His followers, Jn 15:11) is a deep, abiding inner rejoicing in God and giving thanks to God for all His goodness. It is made possible by the Holy Spirit (Ro 14:17; 1 Th 1:6) and is unrelated to circumstances, as is clear from Paul's experience (2 Co 6:4-10). Joy and happiness are not the same; the latter may be related to some momentary good fortune or enjoyment.

Peace is an abiding and assured quietness of soul, the opposite of dread or terror, engendered by complete confidence in the all-sufficiency of God. This experience is beyond the comprehension of a natural or carnal man and can "garrison about" the heart and mind (Phil 4:7) in the midst of very difficult circumstances.

If an individual is strong in the love, joy, and peace of God, he will be able to reach out to his neighbor in a more Christlike manner. His relations with others will be characterized by *longsuffering*, evenness of temper or patient endurance when injured by another or tried by circumstances; *gentleness*, kindness, graciousness, a kindly disposition; *goodness*, beneficence, readiness to do good.

There are at least three principles which guide a spiritual Christian's conduct: *faith*, not faith in God for salvation and daily provision but good faith or fidelity or loving trust toward men; *meekness*, a submissive spirit toward God and man—not weakness but controlled strength; *temperance*, self-control as to one's desires and passions.

"Against such (things, not persons) there is no law." Law is not opposed to these Christian virtues. As Lightfoot observes: "Law exists for the purpose of restraint, but in the works of the Spirit there is nothing to restrain."[11]

"Those who belong to Christ Jesus "(preferred reading of the Greek)," in contrast to those under the law, "have crucified the flesh" (the action is in the Greek aorist tense, indicating a once-for-all action). Paul asserted that this had been his experience (2:20), but now he observes that all Galatian believers share this same experience. The old nature was crucified with Christ (Ro 6:6); this fact became positionally true for every believer at the time he accepted Christ. Now he is therefore dead to the law, and his old nature with its passions and lusts is dead. But what is true in principle or true positionally must become true in experience. The believer must bring the outward manifestation of his Christian life into conformity with his inner spiritual possession by reckoning (Ro 6:11).

Of course he cannot achieve such a victory on his own; he requires divine enablement. "If we live by the Spirit" (v. 25; preferred translation) is what Greek students call a first class condition; there is no doubt about the fact. The translation could properly be "Since we live by the

Spirit." We have been born anew by the Spirit, sealed by the Spirit, and indwelt by the Spirit; there is no question but that we live by the Spirit. Then comes the exhortation "Let us also walk by the Spirit." No simple walking is in view here. From implications in the Greek one might be justified in translating it as "Let us walk in step" by the Spirit. In other words, the intimation of regulating our lives and of walking properly in relation to others is present. The step must be bold and firm and enabled by the Spirit.

Verse 26 is somewhat transitional. At the same time it enlarges on implications of walking by the Spirit and intimates a kind of fault in which one might be overtaken (6:1). Paul demonstrates his very great tact in this verse: "Let us not become vainglorious." He links himself with them in temptation and suggests that this sin was not yet actually true of them, even though it may very well have been. *Vainglorious* literally means "empty glory" and may be translated "conceited." Individuals (possibly leaders of factions) seeking more credit and praise than another will *provoke* ("call forth") in another his evil inclinations. The stronger party will provoke the weaker, and the weaker party will envy the one receiving undue and unmerited praise.

The life of Christian liberty is a life of mutual burden-bearing, 6:1-5

Brethren sets the tone for this section. Spiritually motivated people in the fellowship of believers have a responsibility to help the erring brother. There is no question about the guilt of the alleged sinner, for *overtaken*

means caught in the very act, and a *fault* is a serious lapse.
"You who are spiritual" is not ironical phraseology but a
legitimate appeal to individuals who are walking by the
Spirit. *Restore* is a beautiful word, used for the setting of
a dislocated or broken bone and making it useful to the
whole body once more; of course this must be done with
much care.* Here the spiritual are exhorted to bring the
brother back into his rightful place of fellowship in the
body. This is to be done in a spirit of *meekness,* one of the
fruit of the Spirit, not in an attitude of vainglory or a
"better than thou" attitude on the part of those who have
not fallen into sin. "Considering yourself" marks a shift
from the plural to the singular, indicating that restoration
belongs to the church corporately, but there is individual
responsibility in treatment of others in the proper spirit;
and none of us is immune from falling into sin. Therefore
we should all be extremely gentle in dealing with others
who have capitulated to temptation.

"Restore" of verse 1 must be connected with "bear" in
verse 2. If we are to restore others to full usefulness in the
body of Christ, we shall have to help bear their burdens.
Verse 2 makes a generalization based on the specific situation of verse 1 and certainly includes more than aid to the
erring. *Burdens* are weights too heavy for individuals to
shoulder and capable of being shared with other brethren
in the fellowship of believers. Here is a charge to those
who have sought to carry the wrong kind of burdens (law-
keeping) to assume another burden of the right sort. "Ful-
fil the law of Christ" is to fill up completely the law of

*For other significances of the word translated "restore" see Matthew
4:21 (translated "mending") and Ephesians 4:12 (translated "perfect-
ing").

Christ the burden of which is love (Gal 5:14; Jn 13:34; 15:12). The law of Christ may also be viewed as including all of the self-sacrifice of Christ. At any rate, there is a very real sense in which the believer is *in law* to Christ (see original of 1 Co 9:21), and thus is subject to a person rather than a series of commands.

"Self-conceit, the chief hindrance to forbearing sympathy towards our fellow-men, must be laid aside."[12] If anyone in his own mind thinks himself "to be something" because he has not fallen into sin or is "not as other men are" (Lk 18:11), "when he is nothing he deceives himself." The believer is entirely dependent on the grace of God for salvation and daily enablement (Jn 15:5). This must be true so no flesh should glory before God (1 Co 1:29). "He deceives himself," he is deceived in his mind and thus conceited without a cause.

Verse 4 gives a remedy for self-conceit: "Let every man put to the test continuously his own work." Work is external and can be tested objectively or at least dispassionately. "His own work" puts emphasis on its own intrinsic value. When compared with another's, his work might come off well; when tested on its own merits it may win no seal of approval. The last part of the verse may be translated: "Then shall he have his ground for glorying about himself alone and not about another." Then if he has any cause for glorying, he shall not do so by lording it over another. Of course this verse does not state or even imply that the one who examines his work will have cause for self-glory. The idea of the context is that an individual may easily deceive himself concerning his abilities and spiritual prowess, but when he steps back and takes an objective look at himself and his achievements pride is shattered. Christ has done it all through the power of His Spirit (see Ro 12:3). It is not necessary, however, to be completely negative at this point. Real satisfaction does come to the faithful Christian worker; he can have "rejoicing in himself" or in his own heart as he evaluates his ministry. And he will rejoice even more over any rewards bestowed at the judgment seat of Christ.

"For every man shall bear his own burden" (v. 5). There is no contradiction between verses 5 and 2; different Greek words appear in the two verses. Rendall observes that the word used here designated the pack usually carried by a porter or soldier on the march, and Christ used it to describe the burden He lays on each of His disciples (Mt 11:30).[13] Commentators appear to be almost unanimous in finding in this verse a reference to the day of judgment when each will be held responsible for his own life and work (Ro 14:12). For seems to look back to verse 4. When a man's work is put to the test finally, he must bear the Lord's evaluation of it. How much wood, hay, and stubble will be consumed? Will there be a "well done"? It does not seem necessary to relegate this burden-bearing entirely to the future, however. There are burdens involving the onus of sin, personal suffering, and responsibility of service that no one can share. Perhaps it would be useful to underscore the latter; we cannot slide out from under our personal Christian responsibilities—whether to live a life characterized by the fruit of the Spirit, or rendering spiritual service.

The life of Christian liberty is a life of liberality, 6:6-10

Most commentators see in verse 6 instruction concerning Christian giving: those taught have a responsibility to support those doing the teaching. But some argue cogently and persuasively that giving is not the subject here. The word translated "communicate" really means "to share with," and "all good things" has a far more general meaning than worldly goods; probably it refers to blessings of the Christian faith. The *Word* is not pontifically taught but learned in the sharing by believers; it is not like human wisdom which may be imparted to others. Of course as the Christian community grew and teachers came to give full time to their ministry, this passage could be applied to material support of teachers.

Verse 6 said, "Let him that is taught in the word share with him that teaches in all good things." Verses 7 and 8 encourage the Galatians to focus their attention on all the good spiritual things in which they should seek to excel. In effect the writer is saying, "You cannot turn up your nose at or snub (mock) God; for what a man keeps on sowing, that very thing shall he reap." This law of life is immutable, whether in the realm of nature or the realm of the Spirit. Whatever you sow you will reap, only you will reap much more of the same, for seed bears fruit.

In verse 8 appears a contrast between two sowers: a carnal man and a spiritually minded man. The carnal man sows in the interests of or to promote his own flesh. Every time he performs some action that caters to his flesh, that action produces an effect on his character; the power of the flesh over him increases. With the stimulation of evil

lusts comes a harvest of inward corruption. Even if cater-
ing to the flesh is only an undue emphasis on material
things the sowing will leave its mark. The spiritually
minded man sows in the interests of or to promote the
spirit; probably not the Holy Spirit but the new nature.
Every time he performs some action in the power of the
Spirit, that action produces an effect on his character; the
power of the Spirit over him increases. With the strengthening of his new nature his life becomes more characterized by the fruit of the Spirit. And while he already pos-
sesses life eternal, there is a sense in which the spiritually
minded man will one day have a fuller realization of eternal life, will "reap life everlasting."

Verse 9 extends encouragement to the spiritually minded
man to continue sowing to the spirit, or perhaps the figure
of watering or cultivating would not be out of line. *Weary*
is better translated "lose heart" or "turn cowards." The
encouragement includes hope of rewards for the Christian.
"In due season," in God's own appointed time, if we do
not slacken our efforts because of weariness, we shall reap.
Reaping may in a limited sense come in this life, but the
full harvest will come in the form of rewards at the judgment seat of Christ.

"So then, as we have season, let us work that which is
good to all, especially to those of the household of faith."
There is a season for harvest (v. 9) and also a season for
sowing; the latter encompasses this whole present life. As
we have this present season we must redeem the time.
"Work that which is good" must have a general reference,
perhaps summing up things alluded to in this context:

bearing the burden of others, sowing to the interests of the spirit, and so forth. Some refer it to kindness. "To all" underscores the fact that Christian love knows no limitation as to object. But Christian love must focus especially on supplying the needs of other believers. It would be a tragedy indeed if believers were to be in obvious want before the world; God would appear to be incapable of caring for His own. "The household of faith" are those whom faith has made members of the "household of God" (Eph 2:19).

6

CONCLUSION: FINAL COUNSEL
CONCERNING JUDAIZERS
6:11-18

The Authorized Version gives a completely inaccurate translation of verse 11. In no sense can Galatians be termed a "large letter." A better rendering would be: "You see with what large letters I have written to you with my own hand." What apparently happened here is that Paul now took the pen from his secretary and wrote the rest of the epistle with his own hand. It is questionable whether the apostle wrote any of his epistles in their entirety by himself. We know that at least in several cases he used a secretary (Ro 16:22; 1 Co 16:21; Col 4:18; 2 Th 3:17). Romans developed shorthand in the first century B.C. and Greeks used it earlier than that. Some have argued that the *large letters* indicate Paul had weak eyesight and that this was his "thorn in the flesh." There is no evidence, however, that there was anything wrong with his eyes; identification of his thorn in the flesh is as much a subject of speculation as ever. Here he placards in large letters a conclusion that points up his emotional state at the moment and the importance he attaches to the message addressed to them. The conclusion reiterates some of his major themes. Large letters may refer to capital letters; the rest of the epistle was probably written in a cursive hand.

In verses 12 and 13 Paul scores the insincerity of Judaizing agitators. They try to "put on a good front" or make a display of religious zeal in the flesh, that is, in outward things such as religious rites. In parading the works of the flesh they were sowing to the flesh (v. 8). "They are compelling you [continuous action] to be circumcised," for a very specific reason: "lest they should suffer persecution for the cross of Christ." They were not concerned about the welfare of believers or the glory of God but only about their own safety and reputation. Interestingly enough, Jewish opposition did not center so much on the preaching of Christ as on His all-sufficiency. The negating of circumcision was a dynamite charge to Jews and almost cost Paul his life on more than one occasion. Why not soften the offense of the cross to the Jews? It would have saved Paul a lot of trouble. And it would save modern Christians a lot of trouble. After all, Christ is a great prophet even in Islam.

Those "who receive circumcision," whether Jews or Gentiles, the circumcision party, did not keep the law. Apparently Paul condemned them here not because they did not do what was impossible anyway but because they did not really try to keep the law. They chose circumcision from the whole body of rites and ordinances and seemed to feel that observing it would compensate for their non-observance of the rest. From verse 13 it becomes clear that the circumcision party pushed its cause not only for

their own safety but "that they may glory in your flesh."
They sought to gain some advantage out of the Gentile
believers, to boast of their success in proselytising Gentiles
and to cause them to submit to a merely fleshly ordinance.

In direct contrast to the Judaizing party who would
"glory in your flesh" and avoid the offence of the cross,
Paul says, "But as for me, perish the thought that I should
glory except in the cross of our Lord Jesus Christ" (v. 14).
What was the object of shame to them is an object of
glorying to him. By including *our* he seeks to link them
with him in proper glorying in Christ's cross. The cross
was the instrument "through which the world stands crucified unto me and I unto the world." Of course the *cross*
represents the crucifixion of Christ. The *world* involves
the world system with its allurements, the flesh with its
carnal desires, and even the world religious systems with
their teaching of salvation by human effort. By means of
the death of Christ all of these things stand positionally
rendered inoperative. So now Paul states, "He will glory
only in the triumph of the cross over his own flesh, where-
by the power of the world over him, and his carnal love
of the world, are both done away."[1]

"For, in view of crucifixion to the world and our present
position in Christ, neither circumcision nor uncircumcision
is anything." Far from being something in which to glory,
neither of these *is* (best Greek texts) *anything*. These may
affect the body but do nothing for the soul (cf. Gal 5:6).
But what is significant is a new creation with new life by
the crucifixion and resurrection. The "new creation" is
not new in terms of time, that is, recent, but new in quality
and different in character from the old. It results from a

creative act of God which introduces man to the blessing
of salvation, implants a new heart within him and imparts
to him a whole new nature.

"And as many as shall walk [contrasted with "as many"
in v. 12] according to this rule [measuring rod or standard
that regulates the actions of men, here referring to the
doctrine, of salvation by faith alone], peace be on them
[obviously the peace of God which comforts and strength-
ens] and mercy [merciful loving-kindness toward those in
distress] and [possibly "even"] upon the Israel of God
[possibly the spiritual seed of Abraham by faith, or the
believing element among the Jews, such as Paul, in contrast to the Judaizers]."

Paul concludes the epistle as he began, asserting his
authority as an apostle. "Don't you Judaizers bother me
any more about my right to speak. I bear the true marks
of apostleship. I have the proof of God working through
me. I bear the marks of stripes and stones on my body,
which are there because of my service to God."

"From henceforth [his position and action vindicated, he
turns to the future] let no man trouble me [distract or dis-
turb by attacks on Paul and by preaching a false gospel]:
for I myself [in contrast to the Judaizers who were afraid
of persecution] bear in my body [as a brand] the marks
of Jesus [Lord does not appear in the best texts; His human name reminds one of His sufferings at the hands of
men]." Paul's readers could hardly forget that some of
these scars had been inflicted in their midst.

Then, after all the sorrow and anxiety the Galatians had
cost him, Paul ends the epistle with "brethren" (it comes
at the end of the verse in the original). Of all the benedic-

tions at the end of Paul's epistles, only this one has this term of endearment. In this way he reminds them of their unity in the faith and their relationship with Jesus Christ.

NOTES

BACKGROUNDS AND OUTLINE

1. Merrill C. Tenney, *Galatians: The Charter of Christian Liberty*, p. 15.
2. A. Souter, s.v., "Galatia," *Hastings Dictionary of the Bible;* William M. Ramsay, *The Church in the Roman Empire Before* A.D. *170*, pp. 75-89.
3. William M. Ramsay, *St. Paul the Traveller and the Roman Citizen*, p. 77.

CHAPTER 1

1. George C. Findlay, "The Epistle to the Gentiles," *The Expositor's Bible*, ed. W. Robertson Nicoll, pp. 5, 819.

CHAPTER 3

1. Frederic Rendall, "The Epistle to the Galatians," *The Expositor's Greek Testament*, ed. W. Robertson Nicoll, 3:154.
2. C. F. Hogg and W. E. Vine, *The Epistle of Paul the Apostle to the Galatians*, p. 54.

CHAPTER 4

1. R. C. H. Lenski, *The Interpretation of St. Paul's Epistles to the Galatians, to the Ephesians, and to the Philippians*, p. 146.
2. Frederic Rendall, "The Epistle to the Galatians," *The Expositor's Greek Testament*, ed. W. Robertson Nicoll, 3:171.
3. A. Lukyn Williams, *The Epistle of Paul the Apostle to the Galatians*, p. 76.
4. Rendall, p. 172.
5. Ibid., p. 176.
6. Lenski, p. 218.
7. Ibid., p. 235.
8. Williams, p. 106.
9. Lenski, p. 247.

121

CHAPTER 5

1. Everett F. Harrison, "The Epistle to the Galatians," *The Wycliffe Bible Commentary*, ed. Charles F. Pfeiffer and Everett F. Harrison, p. 1294.
2. Ibid.
3. Frederic Rendall, "The Epistle to the Galatians," *The Expositor's Greek Testament*, ed. W. Robertson Nicoll, 3:184.
4. Harrison, p. 1295.
5. Rendall, p. 186.
6. Harrison, p. 1296.
7. R. C. H. Lenski, *The Interpretation of St. Paul's Epistles to the Galatians, to the Ephesians, and to the Philippians*, p. 280.
8. Ibid., p. 285.
9. J. B. Lightfoot, *Saint Paul's Epistle to the Galatians*, p. 212.
10. Lenski, p. 289.
11. Lightfoot, p. 213.
12. A. R. Fausset, "The Epistle of Paul the Apostle to the Galatians," *A Commentary on the Old and New Testaments*, ed. Robert Jamieson, A. R. Fausset, and David Brown, 6:395.
13. Rendall, p. 189.

CHAPTER 6

1. Frederic Rendall, "The Epistle to the Galatians," *The Expositor's Greek Testament*, ed. W. Robertson Nicoll, 3:191.

Moody Press, a ministry of the Moody Bible Institute, is designed for education, evangelization and edification. If we may assist you in knowing more about Christ and the Christian life, please write us without obligation to: Moody Press, c/o MLM, Chicago, Illinois 60610.

BIBLIOGRAPHY

Alford, Henry. *The Greek Testament. Vol. III.* Rev. by Everett F. Harrison. Chicago: Moody, 1958.

Beet, Joseph A. *A Commentary on St. Paul's Epistle to the Galatians.* London: Hodder & Stoughton, 1885.

Duncan, George S. *The Epistle of Paul to the Galatians.* New York: Harper, 1934.

Eadie, John. *A Commentary on the Greek Text of the Epistle of Paul to the Galatians.* Edinburgh: T. & T. Clark, 1859.

Ellicott, Charles J. *A Critical and Grammatical Commentary on St. Paul's Epistle to the Galatians.* Andover: Warren F. Draper, 1880.

Fausset, A. R. "The Epistle of Paul the Apostle to the Galatians," *A Commentary on the Old and New Testaments. Vol. VI.* By Robert Jamieson, A. R. Fausset and David Brown. Grand Rapids: Eerdmans, 1945.

Findlay, George G. "The Epistle to the Galatians," *The Expositor's Bible. Vol. 5.* Ed. W. Robertson Nicoll. Grand Rapids: Eerdmans, 1943.

Girdlestone, Robert B. *St. Paul's Epistle to the Galatians.* London: Religious Tract Society, 1912.

Godet, F. *Studies on the Epistles.* London: Hodder & Stoughton, 1889.

Harrison, Everett F. "The Epistle to the Galatians," *The Wycliffe Bible Commentary.* Ed. Charles F. Pfeiffer and Everett F. Harrison. Chicago: Moody, 1962.

Hiebert, D. Edmond. *An Introduction to the Pauline Epistles.* Chicago: Moody, 1954.

Hogg, C. F., and Vine, W. E. *The Epistle of Paul the Apostle to the Galatians.* London: Pickering & Inglis, 1922.

Lenski, R. C. H. *The Interpretation of St. Paul's Epistles to the Galatians, to the Ephesians and to the Philippians.* Columbus: Lutheran Book Concern, 1937.

Lightfoot, J. B. *Saint Paul's Epistle to the Galatians.* London: Macmillan, 1902.

Luther, Martin. *A Commentary on St. Paul's Epistle to the Galatians.* Trans. Theodore Graebner. Grand Rapids: Zondervan, 2d ed., n. d.

Martin, R. P. *1 and 2 Corinthians, Galatians.* Grand Rapids: Eerdmans, 1968.

Packer, James I. "Galatians," *The Biblical Expositor. Vol. III.* Ed. Carl F. H. Henry. Philadelphia: Holman, 1960.

Ramsay, William M. *A Historical Commentary on St. Paul's Epistle to the Galatians.* New York: Putnam, 1900.

Rendall, Frederic. "The Epistle to the Galatians," *The Expositor's Greek Testament. Vol. III.* Grand Rapids: Eerdmans, n. d.

Ridderbos, Herman N. *The Epistle of Paul to the Churches of Galatia.* Grand Rapids: Eerdmans, 1953.

Ross, Alexander. "The Epistle to the Galatians," *The New Bible Commentary.* Ed. F. Davidson, A. M. Stibbs, and E. F. Kevan. Grand Rapids: Eerdmans, 1953.

Stott, John R. W. *The Message of Galatians.* London: Inter-Varsity, 1968.

Tenney, Merrill C. *Galatians: The Charter of Christian Liberty.* Grand Rapids: Eerdmans, 1950.

Williams, A. Lukyn. *The Epistle of Paul the Apostle to the Galatians.* Cambridge: U. Press, 1914.